Harmonica Essentials

Gig Savers Complete Edition

I0804551

Essential Theory

FOR THE DIATONIC HARMONICA

A BASIC GUIDE

by DAVID BARRETT

WWW.MELBAY.COM

Essential Theory

The **Gig Savers®** series has been designed to give studying harmonica players answers to common questions in a brief, affordable, yet informative fashion. **Essential Theory** covers the main body of music knowledge needed by all harmonica players. Please refer to the back of this book for a listing of other harmonica books available within this series.

Understanding Notated Music

Staff: The music staff has five lines. Time moves from left to right on the staff.

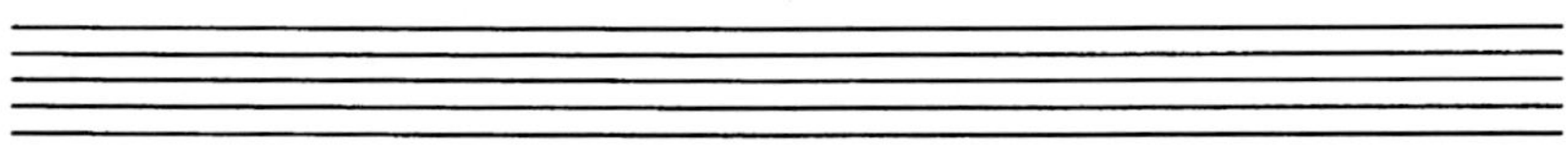

Ledger Lines: The lower lines hold notes that are low in pitch. The upper lines hold notes that are high in pitch. Sometimes notes go beyond the five lines and ledger lines are used to help keep your place.

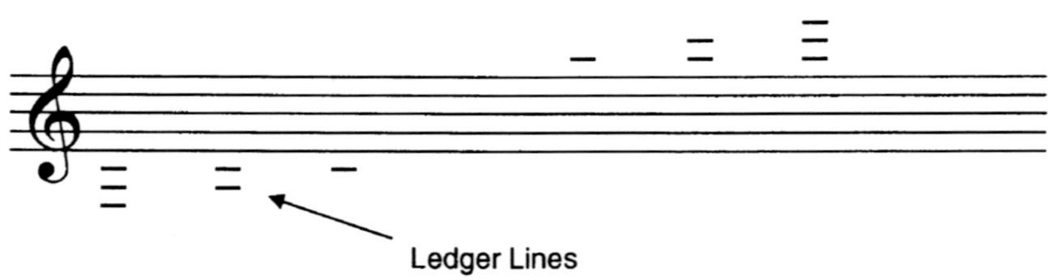

Treble Clef: The treble clef symbol is placed at the beginning of the staff to give a reference pitch. You can see that the bottom curl encircles the second line from the bottom. This second line is the pitch **G**. Because of this, the treble clef is also known as the ***G Clef***.

Notes on the Line: Notes are found on each line of the staff and ledger lines. The notes **E G B D F** found on the staff can be remembered by using "**E**very **G**ood **B**oy **D**oes **F**ine."

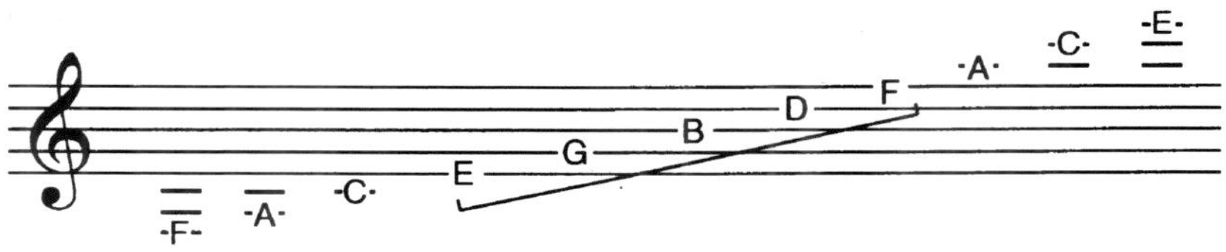

Notes on the Spaces: Notes are also found in the spaces. The notes **F A C E** found on the staff can be remembered by using "**FACE**."

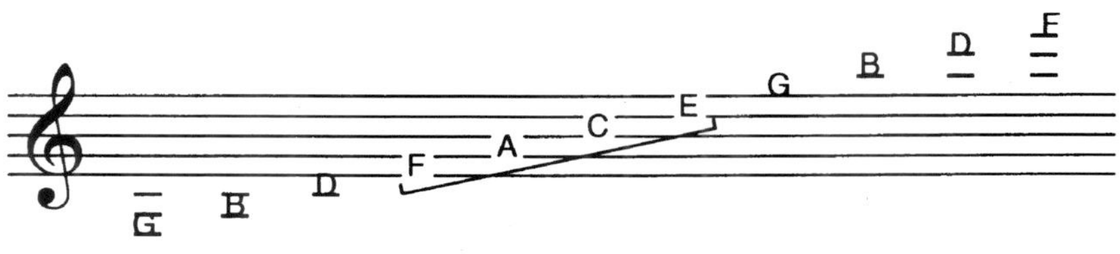

Stem Direction: Notes are placed on these lines and spaces that tell you how long to hold a note. You will see notes that have stems. Some stems point upward and some stems point downward. Stem direction does not change the pitch or length of a note.

Time Signature, Bar Line & Ending: the line that dissects the staff is called a ***Bar Line***. The time between two bar lines is called a ***Measure***. The bar line and thick bar line at the end of the staff tells you that the song is over. The ***Time Signature*** is placed at the beginning of a piece of music to tell you how many beats are in a measure and which note duration is to receive the beat. The 4/4 ***Time Signature*** shows that there are four beats per measure and the quarter note receives the beat.

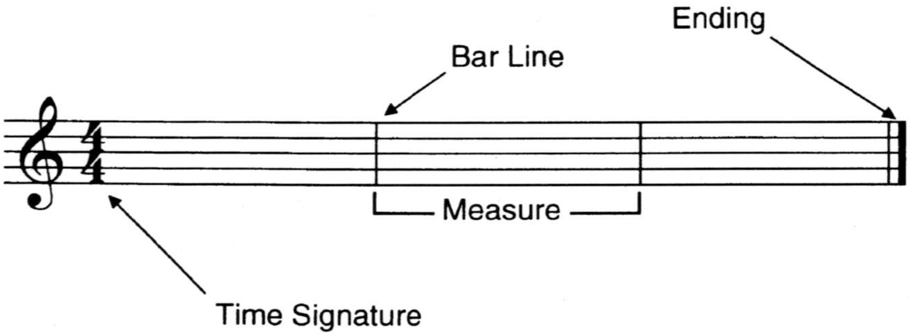

Note Duration: A whole note is held for a count of four beats, or one whole measure. A half note is held for a count of two beats, or half a measure. A quarter note is held for one beat, or one quarter of a measure.

Whole Note Receives 4 Beats	Half Note Receives 2 Beats	Quarter Note Receives 1 Beat

Pitch Duration on the Staff: This example shows: the 4/4 time signature; a **C** whole note for the first measure; a **C** half note and an **A** half note for the second measure; and **B**, **A**, **G**, and **F** quarter notes for the third measure. Notes that subdivide the beat are also used, such as eighth notes and triplets.

4 beats   2 + 2   1 + 1 + 1 + 1

Understanding the Harmonica

The holes of your harmonica are numbered from one to ten. Hole number one (the left end) is the lowest note on the harmonica with the notes getting higher as you slide to the right to number ten. The harmonica can be both blown upon and drawn upon to create a note. For this book we will be using the **C** major diatonic harmonica for demonstration purposes. Your first step in learning the harmonica is to memorize the notes that are available. Diagramed below is the note spread for the **C** major harmonica.

	1	2	3	4	5	6	7	8	9	10
BLOW →	C	E	G	C	E	G	C	E	G	C
C	1	2	3	4	5	6	7	8	9	10
DRAW →	D	G	B	D	F	A	B	D	F	A

Using harmonica tablature to get used to where the placement of notes are on the staff, let's walk through all of the pitches available on the harmonica. Written below are all of the notes found on the harmonica in ascending order. When the hole number is followed by a plus you are to blow (4+ = four blow). When a hole number stands by itself you are to draw (inhale). The example below demonstrates all of the notes naturally available to the **C** major diatonic harmonica. Challenge yourself to learn how to read the music at the same time you are learning the harmonica. Learning it now will allow you to not depend on the harmonica tablature, making sight-reading and the understanding of music concepts much easier.

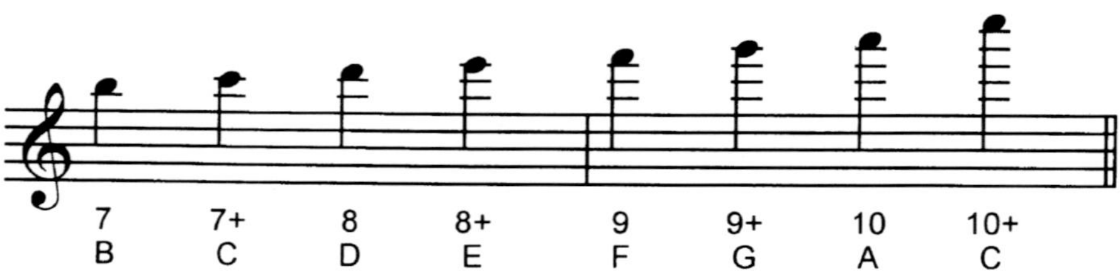

Understanding Scales

Our system of music is based on twelve tones, all equally spaced in pitch by what is called a ***Half Step***. When these twelve tones are placed in ascending or descending order, it is called the ***Chromatic Scale***. Note names start with **A** and go to **G♯**, then those note names repeat, but one octave higher. Detailed below is the chromatic scale from **A** to **A**.

Notice that some of the notes use a sharp (♯). These sharped notes can also be spelled with flats (♭) and retain the same pitch. Example, **A sharp** is the same pitch as **B flat**. You would state that **B flat** is the ***Enharmonic*** of **A sharp**. Detailed below is the same scale with a flat spelling.

Your harmonica is named ***Major Diatonic***. Diatonic denotes the use of a scale that has two half steps and five whole steps. A ***Whole Step*** is the distance of two half steps. Major denotes the placement of the half steps between the second and third notes of the scale and the seventh and eighth notes of the scale. An example of this scale, from **A** is detailed below.

Following this formula of half and whole steps, you can start on any note and create the same sounding scale. The **C** major scale (the scale used on the **C** Major Diatonic Harmonica) is detailed below.

Look at the **C** harmonica note spread below and notice there are some missing scale notes on the lower and upper part of the harmonica.

C	1	2	3	4	5	6	7	8	9	10
BLOW →	C	E	G	C	E	G	C	E	G	C
DRAW →	D	G	B	D	F	A	B	D	F	A

These missing notes can be reclaimed through the use of bending. Detailed below is the **C** harmonica note chart with bending.

C	1	2	3	4	5	6	7	8	9	10
Whole Step Bend (′′) →										B♭
1/2 Step Bend (′) →								E♭	G♭	B
BLOW →	C	E	G	C	E	G	C	E	G	C
DRAW →	D	G	B	D	F	A	B	D	F	A
1/2 Step Bend (′) →	D♭	G♭	B♭	D♭		A♭				
Whole Step Bend (′′) →		F	A							
1-1/2 Step Bend (′′′) →			A♭							

Let's now look at where all these notes are found on the staff.

1+	1'	1	NA	2+	2"	2'	2	3"'	3"	3'	3
C	D♭	D	E♭	E	F	G♭	G	A♭	A	B♭	B

4+	4'	4	NA	5+	5	NA	6+	6'	6	NA	7
C	D♭	D	E♭	E	F	G♭	G	A♭	A	B♭	B

7+	NA	8	8'+	8+	9	9'+	9+	NA	10	10"+	10'+	10+
C	D♭	D	E♭	E	F	G♭	G	A♭	A	B♭	B	C

Understanding Chords

Upon each note of the scale a ***Chord*** can be built. If you play the first, third, and fifth scale degrees together you get the one (**I**) chord. If you play the second, fourth, and sixth scale degrees together you get the two (**ii**) chord. You repeat this process for all of the notes of the scale. Diagramed on the next page are all of the chords available from the **C** major scale.

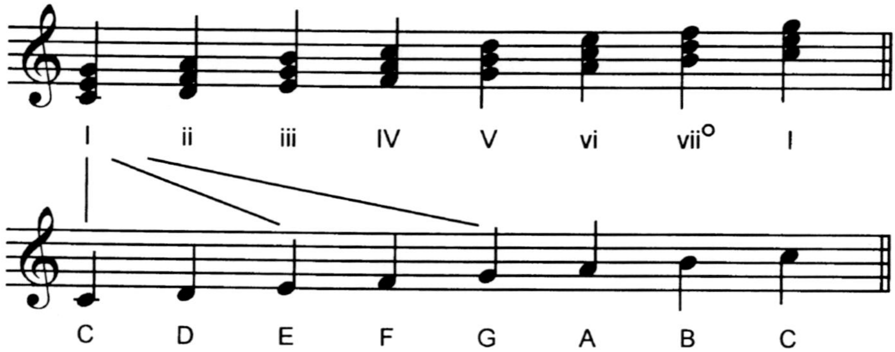

Notice that some chords are designated with an upper case roman numeral and some with lower case. Upper case represents a ***Major Chord*** and lower case represents a ***Minor Chord***. The circle on the seven chord denotes a ***Diminished Chord***.

A ***Major Chord*** is built with two intervals. The distance of the bottom note to the middle note is four half steps; this is called an interval of a ***Major Third***. The middle note to upper note is a distance of three half steps; this is called an interval of a ***Minor Third***. Detailed below is an example of a major chord spelling.

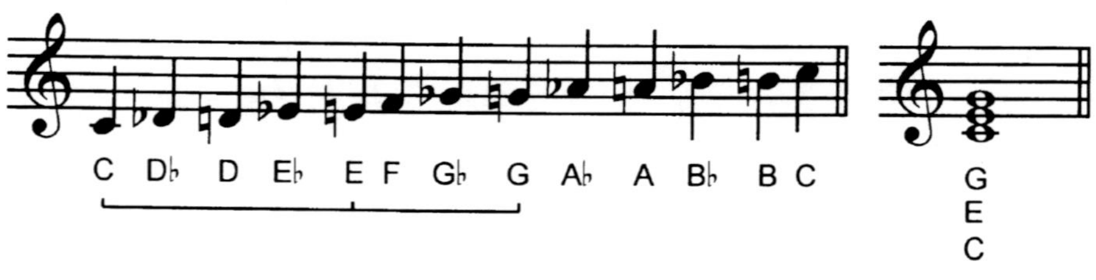

For a ***Minor Chord***, the distance of the bottom note to the middle note is a minor third. The middle note to upper note is a major third. Detailed below is an example of a minor chord spelling.

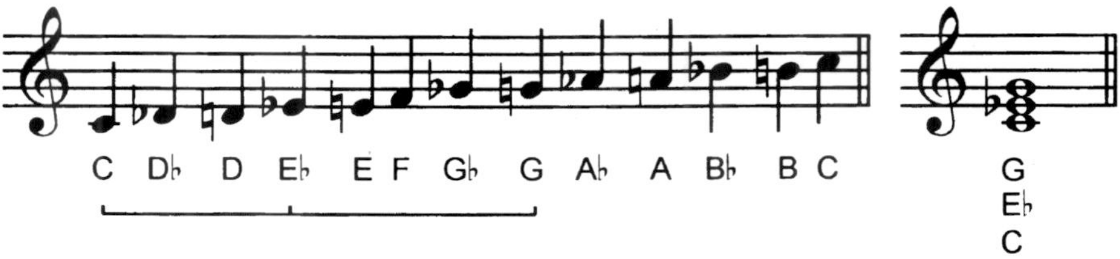

For a ***Diminished Chord***, the distance of the bottom note to the middle note and the middle note to upper note are both minor thirds. Detailed below is an example of a diminished chord spelling.

For an ***Augmented Chord***, the distance of the bottom note to the middle note and the middle note to upper note are both major thirds. Detailed below is an example of an augmented chord spelling.

For Blues, and Blues based forms, one spelling of the seventh chord is commonly used. This is built by using a major chord and placing a note a minor third above the top note. This spelling creates what's called a ***Major-Minor Seventh Chord*** or ***Dominant Seventh Chord***. Detailed on the next page is an example of this chord spelling.

The order of these notes (which note is on bottom, in the middle, etc.) doesn't change the chord's name. By sounding different notes of the chord in the bass (lowest sounding note), you create what are called inversions.

12 Bar Blues

Since most players reading this book play, or will some day play blues, let's take a look at the blues progression. Detailed below is the ***12 Bar Blues Progression***. Slashes on the staff represent each beat of time.

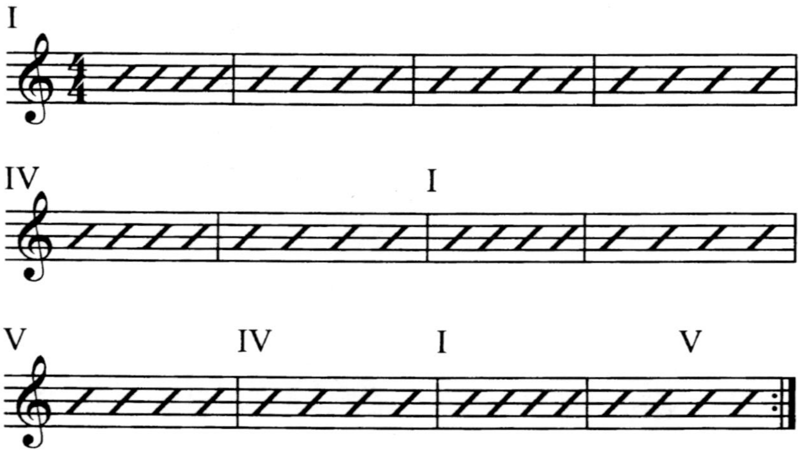

Conventional theory teaches you to know what the notes of the chord are so that you can start with playing those notes to match the band. After understanding the chord and where the notes are found on your harmonica, you can then add other notes of color (non-chord tones) to add interest to your playing. This is good, but most players of blues follow a copy-and-use approach. This is done by listening to a recording, learning a lick (piece of a solo), finding where it fits within the blues progression, and trying to use it yourself. Understanding and hearing the changes of the 12 bar blues is pretty important for either study. To further your knowledge on this subject, I would recommend Mel Bays *Blues Harmonica Jam Tracks & Soloing Concepts* BK/CD #1 (MB99105BCD) and *Exploring 2nd Position* BK/CD (MB99183BCD).

Modes

The major scale, and the chords made from it, is just one scale, or mode available. The major scale is known as the Ionian mode. Listed below are all seven modes. Notice the order of half steps and whole steps change for each scale.

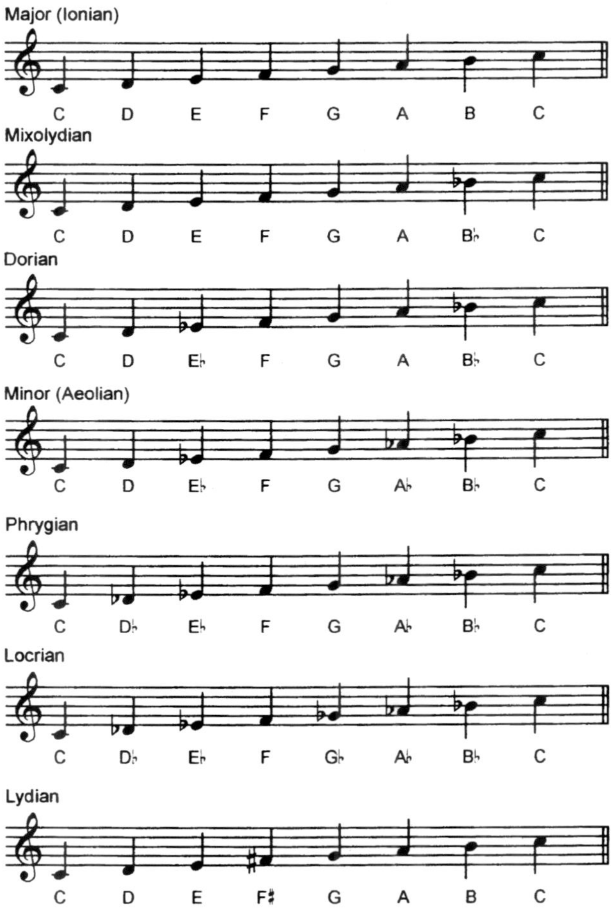

These modes can be used when soloing in a particular key or over a specific chord type. It is good to acquaint yourself with the quality of these chords. Detailed below is how the most commonly used modes differ from the major scale (Ionian).

Major (Ionian) – The most common mode used in American music.

Mixolydian – Flatted seventh scale degree. Very common mode used in blues and popular music. This is the scale naturally available to you (without bending) on the harmonica when playing in second position.

Dorian – Flatted third and seventh scale degrees. Very common mode used in jazz and some blues. This is the scale naturally available to you on the harmonica when playing in third position.

Minor (Aeolian) – Flatted third, sixth and seventh scale degrees. Second most common scale used in American music. Very common mode used in jazz and some blues. This is the scale naturally available to you on the harmonica when playing in fourth position.

Positions

When playing the **C** harmonica in the key of **C**, you are playing in what is called **First Position**. This is the position meant to be played on the harmonica by the designer of the instrument. This position gives you all the notes of the scale and chords by blowing or drawing on more than one hole. One octave of the first position **C** scale on the **C** harmonica is detailed below.

When playing the **C** harmonica in the key of **G**, you are playing in what is called ***Second Position***. This position was developed from the use of bending, which is primarily used on draw notes (First position can also use bending, but is more limited and difficult than second position). The chord that comes from drawing on the harmonica is a **G** chord. The second position **G** scale on the **C** harmonica is detailed below.

When playing the **C** harmonica in the key of **D**, you are playing in what is called ***Third Position***. This position gives you all the notes of the **D *Dorian scale***. The ***Dorian scale*** can be played for a dark sound when playing to a major tune. It also fits very well to minor tunes, being that it has two of the three flatted notes needed to play in minor. One octave of the third position **D** scale on the **C** harmonica is detailed below.

Essential Scales

FOR THE DIATONIC HARMONICA

A BASIC GUIDE

by DAVID BARRETT

Essential Scales

The **Gig Savers®** series has been designed to give studying harmonica players answers to common questions in a brief, affordable, yet informative fashion. **Essential Scales** covers the main body of music knowledge needed by all harmonica players. It is recommended, but not required, that you review **Essential Theory MB20170** before this book. Please refer to the back of this book for a listing of other harmonica books available within this series.

Understanding the Harmonica

The holes of your harmonica are numbered from one to ten. Hole number one (the left end) is the lowest note on the harmonica with the notes getting higher as you slide to the right on number ten. The harmonica can be both blown upon and drawn upon to create a note. For demonstration purposes within this book, we will be using the **C** major diatonic harmonica. Diagramed below is the note spread for the **C** major harmonica.

BLOW →	C	E	G	C	E	G	C	E	G	C
C	1	2	3	4	5	6	7	8	9	10
DRAW →	D	G	B	D	F	A	B	D	F	A

Using harmonica tablature to get used to where the placement of notes are on the staff let's walk through all of the pitches available on the harmonica. Written on the next page are all of the notes found on the harmonica in ascending order. When the hole number is followed by a plus you are to blow (4+ = four blow). When a note stands by itself you are to draw (inhale). The example on the next page demonstrates all of the notes naturally available to the **C** major diatonic harmonica.

1+ 1 2+ 2 3+ 3 4+ 4 5+ 5 6+ 6
C D E G G B C D E F G A

7 7+ 8 8+ 9 9+ 10 10+
B C D E F G A C

Understanding Scales

Our system of music is based on twelve tones, all equally spaced in pitch by what is called a ***Half Step***. When these twelve tones are placed in ascending or descending order, it is called the ***Chromatic Scale***. Note names start with **A** and go to **G**, then these note names repeat, but one octave higher. Detailed below is the chromatic scale from **A** to **A**.

A B♭ B C D♭ D E♭ E F G♭ G A♭ A

Your harmonica is named ***Major Diatonic***. Diatonic denotes the use of a scale that has two half steps and five whole steps. A ***Whole Step*** is the distance of two half steps. Major denotes the placement of the half steps between the second and third notes of the scale and the seventh and eighth notes of the scale. An example of this scale, from **A**, is detailed below.

A B C♯ D E F♯ G♯ A

1/2 Step (C♯–D) 1/2 Step (G♯–A)

Following this formula of half and whole steps, you can start on any note and create the same sounding scale. The **C** major scale (the scale used on the **C** Major Diatonic Harmonica) is detailed below.

Look at the **C** harmonica note spread below and notice there are some missing scale notes on the lower and upper part of the harmonica.

	1	2	3	4	5	6	7	8	9	10
BLOW →	C	E	G	C	E	G	C	E	G	C
C	1	2	3	4	5	6	7	8	9	10
DRAW →	D	G	B	D	F	A	B	D	F	A

These missing notes can be reclaimed through the use of bending. Detailed below is the **C** harmonica note chart with bending.

	1	2	3	4	5	6	7	8	9	10
Whole Step Bend (″) →										B♭
1/2 Step Bend (′) →								E♭	G♭	B
BLOW →	C	E	G	C	E	G	C	E	G	C
C	1	2	3	4	5	6	7	8	9	10
DRAW →	D	G	B	D	F	A	B	D	F	A
1/2 Step Bend (′) →	D♭	G♭	B♭	D♭		A♭				
Whole Step Bend (″) →		F	A							
1-1/2 Step Bend (‴) →			A♭							

Let's now look and see where all these notes are found on the staff.

1+	1'	1	NA	2+	2"	2'	2	3'"	3"	3'	3
C	D♭	D	E♭	E	F	G♭	G	A♭	A	B♭	B

4+	4'	4	NA	5+	5	NA	6+	6'	6	NA	7
C	D♭	D	E♭	E	F	G♭	G	A♭	A	B♭	B

7+	NA	8	8'+	8+	9	9'+	9+	NA	10	10"+	10'+	10+
C	D♭	D	E♭	E	F	G♭	G	A♭	A	B♭	B	C

Position Scales

When playing the **C** harmonica in the key of **C**, you are playing in what is called ***First Position***. This is the position meant to be played on the harmonica by the designer of the instrument. This position gives you all the notes of the scale and chords by blowing or drawing on more than one hole.

The first position ***C Major scale*** on the **C** harmonica is detailed below.

1+	1	2+	2"	2	3"	3	4+
C	D	E	F	G	A	B	C

4+	4	5+	5	6+	6	7	7+
C	D	E	F	G	A	B	C

7+	8	8+	9	9+	10	10'+	10+
C	D	E	F	G	A	B	C

Blues and popular music will commonly lower the seventh note of the scale to create what is called the ***Mixolydian Scale***. This is detailed below.

1+	1	2+	2"	2	3"	3'	4+
C	D	E	F	G	A	B♭	C

4+	4	5+	5	6+	6	NA	7+
C	D	E	F	G	A	B♭	C

7+	8	8+	9	9+	10	10"+	10+
C	D	E	F	G	A	B♭	C

You can also play the ***C Blues Scale*** on the low and high range of the harmonica in first position. This is detailed below.

1+	NA(2+)	2"	2'	2	3'	4+
C	E♭	F	G♭	G	B♭	C

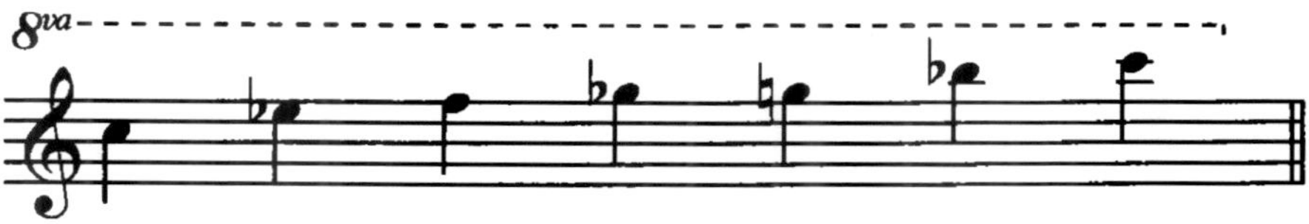

7	8'+	9	9'+	9+	10"+	10+
C	E♭	F	G♭	G	B♭	C

When playing the **C** harmonica in the key of **G**, you are playing in what is called ***Second Position***. This position developed from the use of bending, which is primarily used on draw notes (First position can also use bending, but is more limited and difficult than second position). Detailed on the next page are the two most common soloing scales in this position.

G Mixolydian Scale

NA	NA	NA	1+	1	2+	2"	2
G	A	B	C	D	E	F	G

2	3"	3	4+	4	5+	5	6+
G	A	B	C	D	E	F	G

6+	6	7	7+	8	8+	9	9+
G	A	B	C	D	E	F	G

G Blues Scale

NA	NA	1+	1'	1	2"	2
G	B♭	C	D♭	D	F	G

2	3'	4+	4'	4	5	6+
G	B♭	C	D♭	D	F	G

6+	NA	7+	NA	8	9	9+
G	B♭	C	D♭	D	F	G

When playing the **C** harmonica in the key of **D**, you are playing in what is called ***Third Position***. This position can be played for a dark sound when playing to a major tune. It also fits very well to minor tunes, being that it has two of the three flatted notes needed to play in minor. Detailed on the next two pages are the three most common soloing scales in this position.

D Dorian Scale

1	2+	2"	2	3"	3	4+	4
D	E	F	G	A	B	C	D

4	5+	5	6+	6	7	7+	8
D	E	F	G	A	B	C	D

8	8+	9	9+	10	10'+	10+	NA
D	E	F	G	A	B	C	D

D Blues Scale

1	2"	2	3"'	3"	4+	4
D	F	G	A♭	A	C	D

4	5	6+	6'	6	7+	8
D	F	G	A♭	A	C	D

8	9	9+	NA	10	10+	NA
D	F	G	A♭	A	C	D

D Minor Scale

1	2+	2"	2	3"	3'	4+	4
D	E	F	G	A	B♭	C	D

4	5+	5	6+	6	NA	7+	8
D	E	F	G	A	B♭	C	D

8	8+	9	9+	10	10"+	10+	NA
D	E	F	G	A	B♭	C	D

Lee Oskar Tuned Harmonicas

Many players today play the Lee Oskar system of tuned harmonicas. We'll spend a moment on each of the three tunings (besides the standard major diatonic).

Melody Maker Harmonica

This tuning alters the second position scale to accomodate a complete major scale. Detailed below is a note chart and the ***G Major Scale*** as played on the **G** Melody Maker Harmonica (this harmonica is tuned in second position).

	G									
BLOW →	C	E	A	C	E	G	C	E	G	C
	1	2	3	4	5	6	7	8	9	10
DRAW →	D	G	B	D	F♯	A	B	D	F♯	A

Natural Minor Harmonica

This tuning alters the second position scale to accomodate a complete natural minor scale. Detailed below is a note chart and the ***G Natural Minor Scale*** as played on the **G** Natural Minor Harmonica (this harmonica is tuned in second position as well).

BLOW →	C	E♭	G	C	E♭	G	C	E♭	G	C
G	1	2	3	4	5	6	7	8	9	10
DRAW →	D	G	B♭	D	F	A	B♭	D	F	A

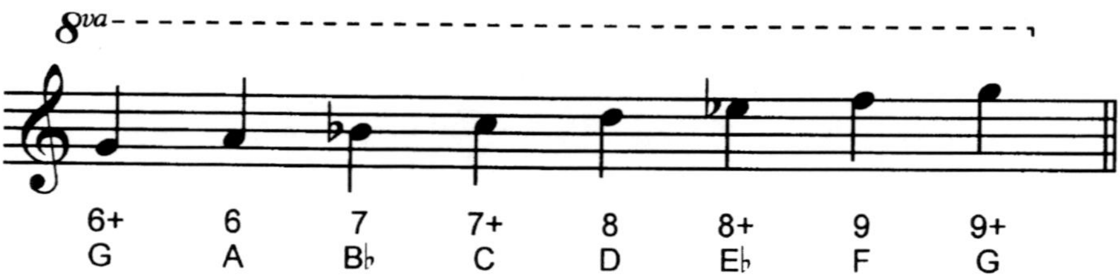

Harmonic Minor Harmonica

This tuning alters the first position scale to accomodate a complete harmonic minor scale (a minor scale with a raised seventh scale degree). Detailed below is a note chart and the **C** Harmonic Minor Scale as played on the **C** Harmonic Minor Harmonica (this harmonica is tuned in first position).

BLOW →	C	E♭	G	C	E♭	G	C	E♭	G	C
C	1	2	3	4	5	6	7	8	9	10
DRAW →	D	G	B	D	F	A♭	B	D	F	A♭

1+	1	2+	2"	2	3'''	3	4+
C	D	E♭	F	G	A♭	B	C

4+	4	5+	5	6+	6	7	7+
C	D	E♭	F	G	A♭	B	C

7+	8	8+	9	9+	10	10'+	10+
C	D	E♭	F	G	A♭	B	C

More Scales for Second Position

Major Diatonic Harmonica

Most readers will spend the majority of their playing time in second position. Here are some additional scales to think about. We'll reference a **C** harmonica playing in second position (key of **G**).

Major Scale

The Major Scale will give you the lightest (non-bluesy) sound when soloing. I recommend that you memorize this scale in its entire range.

Major Pentatonic Scale

From the major scale another scale can be formed, the ***Major Pentatonic Scale***. This scale uses the first, second, third, fifth and sixth scale degrees of the major scale. This is a great scale to use when you want a light sound.

1 2+ 2 2 3" 3 4 5+ 6+
D E G G A B D E G

6+ 6 7 8 8+ 9+
G A B D E G

Mixed Major Pentatonic & Blues Scale

On page 8 you have the entire range of the **G** blues scale notated. After you memorize the blues scale and the major pentatonic scale, you can mix them together. Note the added **A flat** to the scale for a better transition from the low to high end.

When you want a bluesy sound—lean towards the notes of the major scale. When you want a light sound—lean towards the notes of the major scale (or major pentatonic scale). Feel free to play one lick with a bluesy sound, and the next with a light sound. The mixture of different feels can be an exciting effect to use in music, especially for jump and swing blues players (like Little Walter).

1+ 1' 1 2+ 2" 2 3" 3' 3 4+ 4' 4
C D♭ D E F G A B♭ B C D♭ D

5+ 5 6+ 6' 6 7 7+ 8 8+ 9 9+
E F G A♭ A B C D E F G

Essential Quick Charts
FOR THE DIATONIC HARMONICA

A BASIC GUIDE

by DAVID BARRETT

Essential Quick Charts

The **Gig Savers®** series has been designed to give studying harmonica players answers to common questions in a brief, affordable, yet informative fashion. **Essential Quick Charts** gives you all of the important reference charts needed by all players of the instrument. Please refer to the back of this book for a listing of other harmonica books available within this series.

Understanding the Harmonica

Each major diatonic harmonica is tuned to the major diatonic scale. The C major diatonic harmonica uses the C major diatonic scale. The D major diatonic harmonica uses the D major diatonic scale. To play in a different key, all the harmonica player has to do is pick up the corresponding key they want to play in. Because of this, the harmonica player can focus on making music much faster than other instruments. In order for other instruments to play in different keys, they need to learn the note spelling for each of the keys and all of the different fingering patterns for each key. Since the harmonica does this work for us, we can concentrate on making music much sooner. What you play on the C harmonica (patterns, bends, tongue blocked techniques, etc.) does not change for the other harmonicas.

Each of the charts shown to demonstrate a technique, like bending, we will use the C harmonica, knowing that the same technique and movement applies to the other harmonicas. In some sections I will provide you each note for each hole on each keyed harmonica. This does come in handy when playing a B-flat harmonica in third position and the sax player asks what note you are playing! All you know is that you're playing 1 draw. If you go to the chart of the B-flat harmonica, you can see that the note of the 1 draw is C. This is one example of how you can use these charts.

C Harmonica Note Spread

	1	2	3	4	5	6	7	8	9	10
BLOW →	C	E	G	C	E	G	C	E	G	C
C	1	2	3	4	5	6	7	8	9	10
DRAW →	D	G	B	D	F	A	B	D	F	A

C Harmonica Note Spread

	1	2	3	4	5	6	7	8	9	10
Whole Step Bend (″) →										B♭
1/2 Step Bend (′) →								E♭	G♭	B
BLOW →	C	E	G	C	E	G	C	E	G	C
C	1	2	3	4	5	6	7	8	9	10
DRAW →	D	G	B	D	F	A	B	D	F	A
1/2 Step Bend (′) →	D♭	G♭	B♭	D♭		A♭				
Whole Step Bend (″) →		F	A							
1-1/2 Step Bend (‴) →			A♭							

C Harmonica Note Spread With Over-Bends

	1	2	3	4	5	6	7	8	9	10
(OB) Over-Blows →	D♯			D♯		A♯				
(″) Whole-Step Bend / OB					F♯					B♭
(′) Half-Step Bend →								E♭	G♭	B
Blow →	C	E	G	C	E	G	C	E	G	C
Hole → C	1	2	3	4	5	6	7	8	9	10
Draw →	D	G	B	D	F	A	B	D	F	A
(′) Half-Step Bend →	D♭	G♭	B♭	D♭		A♭				
(″) Whole-Step Bend →		F	A				OD → C♯			
(‴) Step & 1/2 Bend →			A♭						OD → G♯	
(OD) Over-Draws →										C♯

Note Spread for All Major Diatonic Harmonicas

	1	2	3	4	5	6	7	8	9	10
C	C	E	G	C	E	G	C	E	G	C
	D	G	B	D	F	A	B	D	F	A

	1	2	3	4	5	6	7	8	9	10
G	G	B	D	G	B	D	G	B	D	G
	A	D	F♯	A	C	E	F♯	A	C	E

	1	2	3	4	5	6	7	8	9	10
D	D	F♯	A	D	F♯	A	D	F♯	A	D
	E	A	C♯	E	G	B	C♯	E	G	B

	1	2	3	4	5	6	7	8	9	10
A	A	C♯	E	A	C♯	E	A	C♯	E	A
	B	E	G♯	B	D	F♯	G♯	B	D	F♯

	1	2	3	4	5	6	7	8	9	10
E	E	G♯	B	E	G♯	B	E	G♯	B	E
	F♯	B	D♯	F♯	A	C♯	D♯	F♯	A	C♯

	1	2	3	4	5	6	7	8	9	10
B	B	D♯	F♯	B	D♯	F♯	B	D♯	F♯	B
	C♯	F♯	A♯	C♯	E	G♯	A♯	C♯	E	G♯

F♯	1	2	3	4	5	6	7	8	9	10
	F♯	A♯	C♯	F♯	A♯	C♯	F♯	A♯	C♯	F♯
	G♯	C♯	E♯	G♯	B	D♯	E♯	G♯	B	D♯

C♯	1	2	3	4	5	6	7	8	9	10
	C♯	E♯	G♯	C♯	E♯	G♯	C♯	E♯	G♯	C♯
	D♯	G♯	B♯	D♯	F♯	A♯	B♯	D♯	F♯	A♯

A♭	1	2	3	4	5	6	7	8	9	10
	A♭	C	E♭	A♭	C	E♭	A♭	C	E♭	A♭
	B♭	E♭	G	B♭	D♭	F	G	B♭	D♭	F

E♭	1	2	3	4	5	6	7	8	9	10
	E♭	G	B♭	E♭	G	B♭	E♭	G	B♭	E♭
	F	B♭	D	F	A♭	C	D	F	A♭	C

B♭	1	2	3	4	5	6	7	8	9	10
	B♭	D	F	B♭	D	F	B♭	D	F	B♭
	C	F	A	C	E♭	G	A	C	E♭	G

F	1	2	3	4	5	6	7	8	9	10
	F	A	C	F	A	C	F	A	C	F
	G	C	E	G	B♭	D	E	G	B♭	D

Position Chart for All Major Diatonic Harmonicas

Harmonica players often play in keys other than what the harmonica is labeled. This is called position playing. ***Second Position*** is the most common. To play in Second Position, you play in a key five scale degrees higher than which it is tuned. Example. You would play a C harmonica in the key of G.

The second most common position is ***Third Position***. To play in Third Position, you play in a key one scale degree higher than it is tuned. Example. You would play a C harmonica in the key of D.

Blues players play in Second Position most of the time, with First and Third Position being less common. Sometimes a melody comes up that can't be played well in First Position (***First Position*** is playing the harmonica in the key it is labeled/tuned). This is where position knowledge comes in handy.

After identifying a song that does not work well in First Position, you would do the following.

1) Find out what key the song is in.
2) Look at the following *Position Chart* to see which harmonicas are options for that key.
3) Look at the notes on each of the harmonicas from the preceeding chart to find out if the notes are readily available.

As an example, let's say the notes below are used.

A C E C E

Using the previous Note Spread for *All Major Diatonic Harmonicas* chart, look at the harmonica options to see what harmonicas you can use?

If you run into a note or two that are not available on a harmonica in a particular key, you could either skip that one and look for another harmonica, or check to see if you can bend some notes to create the pitch(s) you are looking for. Many songs cannot be played without a couple of bent notes.

For our previous example of **A C E C E**. You can use a C harmonica in Fourth Position. You would play: 6 draw, 7 blow, 8 blow, 7 blow, 8 blow. You can also use a G harmonica in Third Position. You would play: 4 draw, 5 draw, 6 draw, 5 draw, 6 draw. What other harmonicas do you see?

Because the major diatonic harmonica is built to really only play in one key, it takes some innovative thinking to bring more possibilities to the table.

Band Key Position Chart

Band Key	Harmonica To Play in This Position											
	1st	2nd	3rd	4th	5th	6th	7th	8th	9th	10th	11th	12th
A♭/G♯	A♭	D♭	F♯	B	E	A	D	G	C	F	B♭	E♭
G	G	C	F	B♭	E♭	A♭	D♭	F♯	B	E	A	D
G♭/F♯	F♯	B	E	A	D	G	C	F	B♭	E♭	A♭	D♭
F	F	B♭	E♭	A♭	D♭	F♯	B	E	A	D	G	C
E	E	A	D	G	C	F	B♭	E♭	A♭	D♭	F♯	B
E♭/D♯	E♭	A♭	D♭	F♯	B	E	A	D	G	C	F	B♭
D	D	G	C	F	B♭	E♭	A♭	D♭	F♯	B	E	A
D♭/C♯	D♭	F♯	B	E	A	D	G	C	F	B♭	E♭	A♭
C	C	F	B♭	E♭	A♭	D♭	F♯	B	E	A	D	G
B	B	E	A	D	G	C	F	B♭	E♭	A♭	D♭	F♯
B♭/A♯	B♭	E♭	A♭	D♭	F♯	B	E	A	D	G	C	F
A	A	D	G	C	F	B♭	E♭	A♭	D♭	F♯	B	E

How to Use this Chart

Select band key on left. Choose which position you would like to play that key in. Use your finger to follow the chosen position down until you see the correct band key on the left. Your finger will be over the harmonica you will need to use.

Example. Band is in the key of F. You want to play in 2nd position. Look down the 2nd position column until you see the key of F on the left. The key of harmonica needed is a B♭ harmonica to play in the key of F in 2nd position.

Harmonica Key Position Chart

HARP Key	Band Key if Played in this Position											
	1st	2nd	3rd	4th	5th	6th	7th	8th	9th	10th	11th	12th
A♭	A♭	E♭	B♭	F	C	G	D	A	E	B	F♯	D♭
G	G	D	A	E	B	F♯	D♭	A♭	E♭	B♭	F	C
F♯	F♯	D♭	A♭	E♭	B♭	F	C	G	D	A	E	B
F	F	C	G	D	A	E	B	F♯	D♭	A♭	E♭	B♭
E	E	B	F♯	D♭	A♭	E♭	B♭	F	C	G	D	A
E♭	E♭	B♭	F	C	G	D	A	E	B	F♯	D♭	A♭
D	D	A	E	B	F♯	D♭	A♭	E♭	B♭	F	C	G
D♭	D♭	A♭	E♭	B♭	F	C	G	D	A	E	B	F♯
C	C	G	D	A	E	B	F♯	D♭	A♭	E♭	B♭	F
B	B	F♯	D♭	A♭	E♭	B♭	F	C	G	D	A	E
B♭	B♭	F	C	G	D	A	E	B	F♯	D♭	A♭	E♭
A	A	E	B	F♯	D♭	A♭	E♭	B♭	F	C	G	D

How to Use this Chart

Select harmonica key on left. Choose which position you would like to play that key harmonica in. Use your finger to follow the chosen position down until you see the correct harmonica key on the left. Your finger will be over the band key you will need to call.

Example. You have a B♭ harmonica. You want to play this harmonica in second position. Look down the 2nd position column until you see your harmonica at left. Your finger will be over the band key of F. The B♭ harmonica in 2nd position plays in the key of F.

Note Spread for Lee Oskar Tuned Harmonicas

C Major Diatonic Harmonicas (Same)

Labeled in First Position

BLOW →	C	E	G	C	E	G	C	E	G	C	
C	1	2	3	4	5	6	7	8	9	10	
DRAW →	D	G	B	D	F	A	B	D	F	A	

G Melody Maker Harmonica

Labeled in Second Position

BLOW →	C	E	A	C	E	G	C	E	G	C	
MM	1	2	3	4	5	6	7	8	9	10	G
DRAW →	D	G	B	D	F♯	A	B	D	F♯	A	

G Natural Minor Harmonica

Labeled in Second Position

BLOW →	C	E♭	G	C	E♭	G	C	E♭	G	C	
N	1	2	3	4	5	6	7	8	9	10	Gm
DRAW →	D	G	B♭	D	F	A	B♭	D	F	A	

C Harmonic Minor Harmonica

Labeled in First Position

Cm	1	2	3	4	5	6	7	8	9	10	H
BLOW →	C	E♭	G	C	E♭	G	C	E♭	G	C	
DRAW →	D	G	B	D	F	A♭	B	D	F	A♭	

Bend Charts for Lee Oskar Tuned Harmonicas

G Melody Maker Harmonica

MM	1	2	3	4	5	6	7	8	9	10	G
Whole Step Bend (″) →										B♭	
1/2 Step Bend (′) →								E♭		B	
BLOW →	C	E	A	C	E	G	C	E	G	C	
DRAW →	D	G	B	D	F♯	A	B	D	F♯	A	
1/2 Step Bend (′) →	D♭	G♭	B♭	D♭	F	A♭					
Whole Step Bend (″) →		F									

G Natural Minor Harmonica

	N	1	2	3	4	5	6	7	8	9	10	Gm
Whole Step Bend (″) →											B♭	
1/2 Step Bend (′) →								B		G♭	B	
BLOW →		C	E♭	G	C	E♭	G	C	E♭	G	C	
DRAW →		D	G	B♭	D	F	A	B♭	D	F	A	
1/2 Step Bend (′) →		D♭	G♭	A	D♭	E	A♭					
Whole Step Bend (″) →			F	A♭								
1-1/2 Step Bend (‴) →			E									

C Harmonic Minor Harmonica

	Cm	1	2	3	4	5	6	7	8	9	10	H
1-1/2 Step Bend (‴) →											A	
Whole Step Bend (″) →											B♭	
1/2 Step Bend (′) →										G♭	B	
BLOW →		C	E♭	G	C	E♭	G	C	E♭	G	C	
DRAW →		D	G	B	D	F	A♭	B	D	F	A♭	
1/2 Step Bend (′) →		D♭	G♭	B♭	D♭	E						
Whole Step Bend (″) →			F	A								
1-1/2 Step Bend (‴) →			E	A♭								

All Notes of Major Scales

Key	Major Scale							
A♭	A♭	B♭	C	D♭	E♭	F	G	A♭
G	G	A	B	C	D	E	F♯	G
G♭	G♭	A♭	B♭	C♭	D♭	E♭	F	G♭
F♯	F♯	G♯	A♯	B	C♯	D♯	E♯	F♯
F	F	G	A	B♭	C	D	E	F
E	E	F♯	G♯	A	B	C♯	D♯	E
E♭	E♭	F	G	A♭	B♭	C	D	E♭
D	D	E	F♯	G	A	B	C♯	D
D♭	D♭	E♭	F	G♭	A♭	B♭	C	D♭
C♯	C♯	D♯	E♯	F♯	G♯	A♯	B♯	C♯
C	C	D	E	F	G	A	B	C
B	B	C♯	D♯	E	F♯	G♯	A♯	B
B♭	B♭	C	D	E♭	F	G	A	B♭
A	A	B	C♯	D	E	F♯	G♯	A

All Notes of Minor Scales

Key	Minor Scale							
A♭	A♭	B♭	C♭	D♭	E♭	F♭	G♭	A♭
G	G	A	B♭	C	D	E♭	F	G
F♯	F♯	G♯	A	B	C♯	D	E	F♯
F	F	G	A♭	B♭	C	D♭	E♭	F
E	E	F♯	G	A	B	C	D	E
E♭	E♭	F	G♭	A♭	B♭	C♭	D♭	E♭
D	D	E	F	G	A	B♭	C	D
C♯	C♯	D♯	E	F♯	G♯	A	B	C♯
C	C	D	E♭	F	G	A♭	B♭	C
B	B	C♯	D	E	F♯	G	A	B
B♭	B♭	C	D♭	E♭	F	G♭	A♭	B♭
A	A	B	C	D	E	F	G	A

Diatonic to Chromatic Harmonica Reference

C	1	2	3	4	5	6	7	8	9	10
BLOW →	C	E	G	C	E	G	C	E	G	C
DRAW →	D	G	B	D	F	A	B	D	F	A

C	1	2	3	4	5	6	7	8	9	10
	C	E	G	C	C	E	G	C	C	E
	D	F	A	B	D	F	A	B	D	F

C	1	2	3	4	5	6	7	8	9	10	11	12
	C	E	G	C	C	E	G	C	C	E	G	C
	D	F	A	B	D	F	A	B	D	F	A	B

C	$\dot{1}$	$\dot{2}$	$\dot{3}$	$\dot{4}$	1	2	3	4	5	6	7	8	9	10	11	12
	C	E	G	C	C	E	G	C	C	E	G	C	C	E	G	C
	D	F	A	B	D	F	A	B	D	F	A	B	D	F	A	B

Harmonica Microphones

A BASIC GUIDE

by DAVID BARRETT
& FRITZ HASENPUSCH

Live photo of David Barrett
by
Sarbajit Banerjea

Harmonica Microphones

The **Gig Savers®** series has been designed to give studying harmonica players answers to common questions in a brief, affordable, yet informative fashion. ***Harmonica Microphones*** is the first published book to specifically cover harmonica microphones (mics) and their usage. This is a subject of special interest to all harp (harmonica) players due to the lack of available information on this topic – until now. Most players, like myself, have had to acquire many mics and amps in the pursuit of finding the magic combination that would furnish the desired sound. I have personally owned over one hundred different mics of various models. As a result, I've gathered a great deal of first-hand information on their use that will be shared through this book. Coauthor Fritz Hasenpusch is an expert on the subject; building and working on thousands of mics for customers around the world.

Although this publication is primarily written for the blues harp player, it contains plenty of information that will prove useful to the non-blues player as well. Please refer to the back of this book for a listing of other harmonica books available within this series. I highly recommend purchasing the book ***Harmonica Amplifiers*** as well to round out your knowledge of the subject, since the mic is only half of the electronic equation for achieving the tone you seek.

I would like to thank Sonny Junior of Sonny Junior Amplifiers, Fritz Hasenpusch (Fritz the Harp Mic Man), and Tom Ellis of Tom's Mics for their expert information and help through the years.

The Package

The two most important aspects of a mic are how it sounds and how it feels in your hands. The microphonic element (also known as the cartridge or capsule) picks up your sound and sends the electronic signal to the amplifier (amp). The mic elements preferred by players over the years are relatively large in diameter, requiring mic grills and bodies somewhat larger than many players might choose. Keep in mind these classic mics were never intended to be held in the hands, and harp players have improvised this use. It is a balance between these aspects of the "package" that harp players are looking for: A mic that looks nice, feels good in the hands and sounds great.

The Body & Element

The body (or shell) of the microphone has one main design purpose: to act as the enclosure for its electronic components (the element, transformer, volume control, on/off switch, wiring, output connector, etc.). But for our purposes, the body's shape provides the contours that will allow the player to "cup" all the sound from the harp directly into the mic's element via its frontal grill. To this function, the bullet-shaped microphone, born of the art-deco design movement, works very well.

Note the microphone pictured on the next page (Shure 520). Sound can only enter through the frontal grill, making cupping fairly easy. By comparison, the microphone pictured at its right (Electro-Voice Mercury) is virtually all grill, making cupping (and directing pressure into the element) nearly impossible.

Shure 520 Bullet

Electro-Voice Mercury

In addition to being "cup friendly," bullet mics owe much of their popularity to the large diameter elements that many models came equipped with. Over the years since their early development, several of these elements have proven to produce "harp-friendly" tone.

Keep this in mind when we discuss "tone:" "Good tone" is a subjective matter. Mic and amp choices are based upon general preferences in sound and are a matter of individual taste, and taste can vary dramatically. Historically, most blues harp players have used a variety of makes and models of the bullet mic design. Other designs have been used as well (wand, ball, pistol, etc.) and these will be investigated too.

Let's start our journey into the different makes and models of mics and learn what they look and sound like.

Shure Microphones

This is one of the most popular microphone brands, with many models that have been popular choices for their "packages" of shape, size, looks and sound.

7A Body Style – This body was the first Shure microphone produced (1939) that carries the well-known bullet shape in its pure

form (A screw-on output connector has been added to this mic. The 7A originally had a cable that went out the rear in the same location). It was preceded to market by the Shure 705A "Rocket." Though nearly a bullet, its fins, pivoting stand mount, and bulbous grill render it less desirable for harp applications (though it remains highly collectable). Most players are familiar with the later Shure 520 "green bullet" body size, which is a bit larger and heavier than the 7A. These earlier incarnations with smaller bodies have a diameter of 2-3/8" and length of 2-7/8", whereas the newer 520 body size (1949 on) has a diameter of 2-15/32" and a length of 3-1/4". The earlier/smaller Shure bullet is a highly preferred body size by many players. Although the 7A itself is very rare, bodies made from the same mold came in other models that are more readily available. Some examples are: Model 18-51 "Specially Designed for Recording," and some similar examples with no names or numbers visible on them at all. Collectively, these microphones are referred to as the "Brown Bullets" due to their being finished in varying shades of brown. The case of the long-lived 707 model is often referred to as the "Silver Bullet," for obvious reasons.

Nearly all of these mics (to my knowledge) came with ***Crystal Elements*** (the exception being the rare 1939 5E, which came with a dynamic element). These old crystal elements sound fantastic when healthy, but are VERY rarely found in good working order. Reason? Crystal elements by nature are very delicate, and subject to deterioration due to heat, moisture and impact. Over time they simply dissolve. I have personally owned over forty Shure mics with crystal elements and the few that were working were either weak in tone (low signal) or performed great for five minutes and then died. I have had only two that enduringly worked well over a long period of time, producing a strong signal.

If you were to compare a healthy Shure crystal to the newer Astatic crystals, you would find they have a strong bass response and "presence" to them, more similar to that found in the larger Shure Controlled-Reluctance and Controlled Magnetics Elements.

520 Body Style – In 1949 the 520 body replaced the smaller-bodied bullets. Almost identical in design (besides the proportionate size and weight gain), these mics have been the mainstay of many players. As with their smaller-bodied predecessors, these newer mics also had many model names. According to Shure's archives the 520 was made from 1949-1977, the 440 from 1960-1970, and the 707 from 1940-1970. The 707A carried the same model name for the older-smaller body as well as the newer-larger body. One way to tell their age is by looking at the grill. All of the smaller/older bullets I've encountered (with the exception of one older mic I came across) have their grill lines running top to bottom. The newer/larger-bodied mics have their grill lines running left to right.

In their early years, these 520 bodies had a ***Controlled-Reluctance (CR)*** element. This is a much hardier element than its fragile crystal predecessors, not nearly as sensitive to damage from dropping, heat, or moisture. Designed for "high speech intelligibility" in communications mics, when applied to the amplification of harp, they yield a tone that's "big" and "strong," with a full round sound.

Though the name was later changed to ***Controlled Magnetic (CM)***, these two elements were presumably produced on the same equipment with minor changes to design, materials, and assembly over the years. In comparison, the CR element is slightly hotter in output, yielding a more overdriven sound. The newer CM's are commonly a bit smoother in response. Though comparisons between any CR and CM elements could yield different results, just remember that they are both capable of sounding fantastic for harp.

Note: Be aware that when shopping for a microphone equipped with a CR or CM element, you should look for units that are ***High Impedance****. These will work with typical instrument amplifiers without the need for an external impedance-matching transformer, as necessitated by units that are* ***Low Impedance****.*

After production of the 520 stopped in 1977, there was a period where no Shure bullets were made. Some years back, Shure recreated the 520 as the 520D, manufactured in Mexico. The 520D has since (~1998) been discontinued as a result of the wear on the tooling for CM element production. It has since been replaced by the 520DX. The new member of the 520 family has a handy volume control and employs a large diameter ***Dynamic Element*** *(pictured above)* derived from Shure's communications microphones. This element is just as hardy as the CM predecessor, but has a broader, flatter response curve, yielding more audible "highs." For some amps, this is a positive difference. For other amps, not as good.

Reminder: Try as many mics as you can with an amp you especially like. You may find workable combinations that will surprise you.

Interchangeability of Shure Elements

All elements common to bullet mics mentioned thus far will fit in either Shure bullet body size, although some gasket modification will be necessary. Also know that the older Shure elements will fit in most Astatic shells (as Astatic elements will fit in most Shure bullet shells).

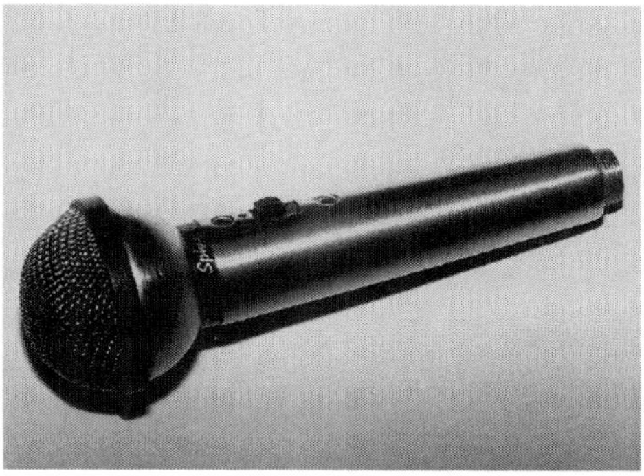

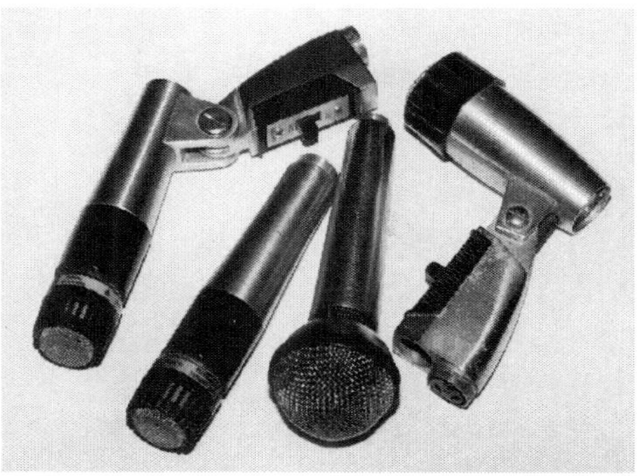

533SA (1965-1984) is a great example of the Shure dynamic microphone family used by harp players. This model, commonly known as the "Sphere-O-Dyne," was first introduced to me by mic expert Tom Ellis. What a wonderful sounding mic – a definite option for the non-bullet lovers or those on the hunt for a new sound. Notice that the mic's grill does not encompass the entire "ball" of the mic, making cupping easier. Shure dynamics, such as the 545 Unidyne, both "pistol" (pictured left) and "wand" (pictured left-center) styles (used by Paul Butterfield), 540 (pictured right) and 533 models are all good options if you are looking for something a little different or merely want to add some variety to your sound.

Astatic Microphones

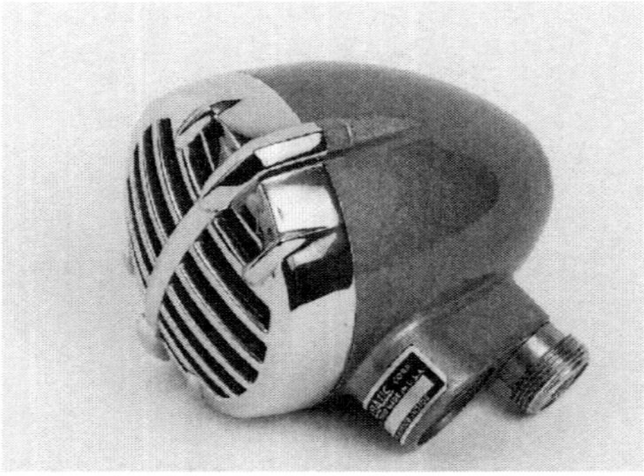

JT-30 – Like Shure, Astatic has been a microphone mainstay in the blues world for harp players. Developed in the early 30's, the JT-30 (pictured at left) has been the most notable of their product line. Equipped with a strong crystal element (most recently the MC-151), it is a wonderful-sounding and highly versatile mic. As with the Shure bullet mics, the Astatic JT-30 has been marketed under a variety of model names, sometimes with minor variations in design or finishing details. With few exceptions they did all share the same grill, body shell and element. The most noticeable variations over the years have been the color of their painted finishes, output connectors, and absence or addition of volume controls.

The one variation that you couldn't see was the offering of the MC-127 ***Ceramic Element*** in the JT-30-C. The ceramic element was developed to deliver a response similar to the crystal but without the fragilities that crystals are infamous for (the ceramics do last longer and are more stable). The MC-127 ceramic element is preferred by some harp players for its smoother, somewhat darker response (though I personally like the brighter, harder edge that the Astatic crystal element provides).

The newer models based on the JT-30 had been marketed by Astatic, CAD, Hohner, and other private labels and came with XLR output connectors (standard three-pin pro audio connectors) and volume controls mounted towards the bottom-rear of the stand lug.

Note. When buying a cable for these mics, make sure the cable you purchase is wired in the unconventional "3-Pin Hot," 2-pin empty configuration, not in the typical pro audio fashion (3-return, 2-hot, 1-ground) as this simply won't work. Many a player has mistakenly thought his mic had died when in fact he'd been sold a miswired cable by a misinformed salesman (who was probably a guitarist! A little harmonica humor).

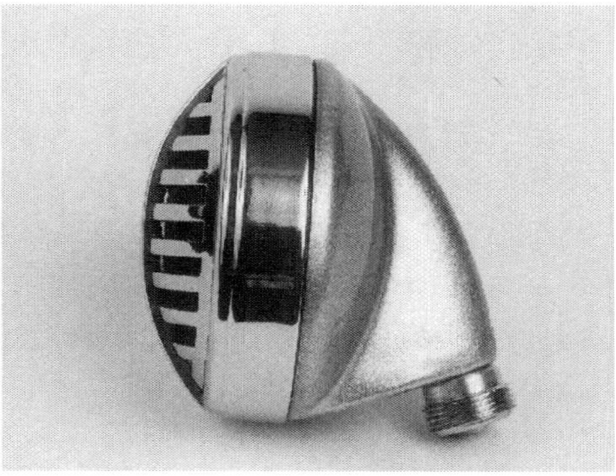

Model 30 "Biscuit"–This is a wonderful option for the bullet user (A screw-on output connector has been added to this mic. This mic originally had a cable that exited the shell in the same location). Notice the large diameter and the unusual proportions. The advantage of this body type is its lighter weight and ease of holding due to the smooth unornamented grill and shallow body depth. Like other mics we've discussed, the "biscuit" can house any of the popular Astatic or Shure elements (except for the Shure 520DX element). Although not seen as often in players' hands as the JT-30 or Shure bullets, many knowledgeable performers like William Clarke and Tom Ball have found the advantages of "the biscuit."

Other models by Astatic have been used by harp players, as well. The sleek T3 is smaller that the JT-30, shaped like an all-chrome goose egg, and wired through a pivoting stand connector.

The 200 series has a conical bullet head with an integrally cast handle/stand mount. Although a bit awkward, it employs the same electronics as the more popular Astatics. Many examples of this model employ a flat profile grill that can be an advantage in cupping. The 200 is often modified by mic customizers who remove the mic's head from the handle and install an output connector (an XLR fits perfectly) in the resulting hole. Among others, Charlie Musselwhite and Annie Raines have been photographed performing using this mic in its stock form.

Electro-Voice, Turner & Others

What we've covered so far are the most common mics used in the past and the present. Besides them, there are many, many other models that can be used to a harp player's advantage. Here are some examples of mics that are less commonly seen, but cool none-the-less.

Turner Challenger - The Turner family of microphones really adds a deco touch to a players collection. Most of the microphones came with the high-impedance dynamic cartidge pictured here or a crystal cartridge. The dynamic cartridge is a little wider and smoother in its response compared to a Shure CM. These mics are a nice balance for amps that tend to distort easily. Some players stay away from the Turner models with protruding fins (model 22, for example). Most experienced players can overcome this, however. Come in Buck Rogers!

Of the more cup-friendly Turners, the **BX** models are crystal; **BD** models dynamic; **CX** models are the same as the **BX**, but with a satin chrome finish like the one pictured; **CD** models use dynamic cartridges with what they call "a high quality magnet" and seems to have a stronger output than the others.

Electro-Voice 605 – The EV line of mics offers some strong candidates for consideration. With mostly dynamic elements and smaller body-styles (though heavy), they are also nice alternatives to the standard bullet body and produce a distinct sound. The 605, 638, 920, 630, 620, 641, and 607 are all workable models for the harpist.

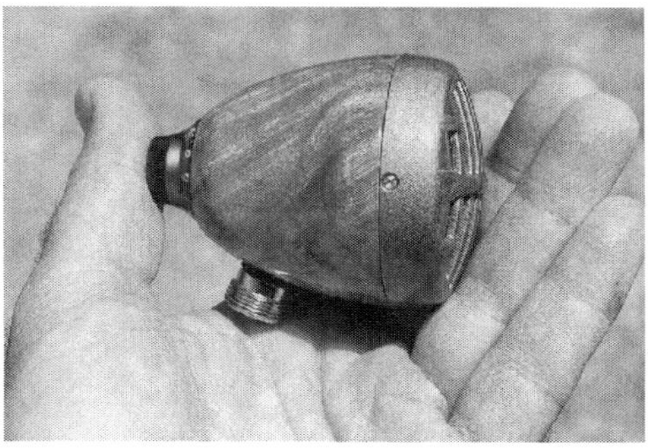

Custom Microphones – Here is an example of a custom microphone from Fritz Hasenpusch. It employs a JT30 grill with its ornamental lugs taken off, beautifully carved and finished wood body, and an innovative use of a volume control and custom screw-on output connector. From taking odd bodies and making them more usable for the harmonica player, to fully custom mics like this one, the options and possibilities are limitless.

Accessories

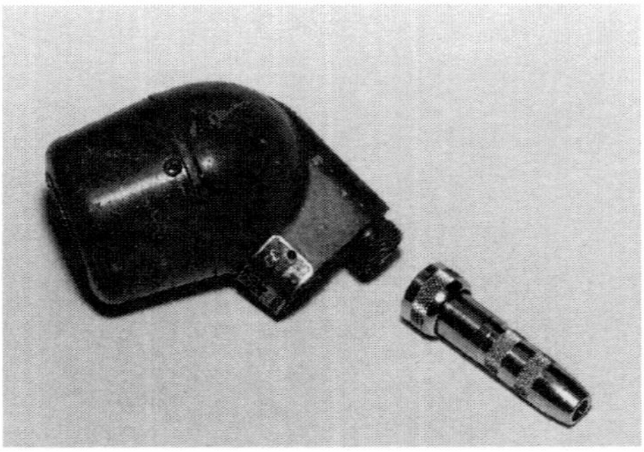

Many accessories and options are available for harmonica mics, both vintage and new. I personally have all of my microphones fitted with A ***Screw-On Output Connector*** (Switchcraft 2501MP). This way I only need one type of cable, but I can carry many microphones to a gig if I wish. Switchcraft also makes a screw-on to 1/4" female adapter (332A, pictured above with an early original Electro-Voice 605) so you can use a standard 1/4" instrument cable instead of a specialty cable if you wish.

Some players leave the cable in the back hole of the hard-wired Shure bullets, cut it off short and install a female 1/4" connector on the end so they can use a standard instrument cable. Where internal dimensions allow, you can also drill a hole in the recessed microphone stand mount area and install a 1/4" guitar jack. Many others and I have done this, but be aware that it's easy to step on your cable during a performance and pull it out. I also found that the nut that holds the jack in place would often become loose, resulting in grounding problems.

Volume Controls can also be useful tools when added to a harmonica microphone. Volume controls are primarily used to turn the mic's level down during background and support
playing, and up during featured and solo playing. It's also handy for turning the mic off when it's not in use (when you're "sitting-out," between sets or singing).

Volume controls, or "pots" (short for potentionmeters) can be placed anywhere on the mic that internal space will allow, and are most commonly positioned through the mic's threaded stand mount at its bottom. A benefit of this placement is that the knob protrudes less than a surface mounting, and you preserve the mic's exterior as well by not drilling holes you might later regret. This installation involves drilling the appropriate size hole through the floor of the 5/8" stand mount hole and re-wiring the internals to accomodate the new pot. Note: Make sure that any "mods" are properly grounded.

External "in-line" volume controls can be utilized and can help avoid the boring of holes in a prized microphone. Pictured above is a very rare and collectible in-line volume control (Switchcraft 329) designed for mics that use "Amphenol" thread-on connectors (2501). Less exotic models are available in foot-pedal form. Connected/placed between your microphone and amp, the volume pedal operates on the same principle as a volume control on the mic, merely foot actuated. Mark Ford and other notable harp players use a foot pedal volume control.
Note: Always make certain any added electronic components are compatible with the mic's element; impedence values vary.

Many players prefer an ***On/Off Switch*** in place of a volume control. My mentor, Gary Smith, would always play with his amp on the verge of feedback. He would achieve great tone this way, but to stop unwanted feedback produced when not playing, Gary would switch the mic off just before pulling his hands away from his face, and switch it back on just as he'd begin to play again.

Notes on Modification

1. Make sure that all electronic parts are compatible and properly grounded.
2. Be careful not to leave the solder gun's tip on any element or component too long. This is particularly important when dealing with heat-sensitive crystal elements.
3. When mixing and matching elements and bodies, expect there to be some gasket work to assure proper fit and seal between element and body.
4. When placing a Shure CM or CR element in a microphone body with any rear/shell openings, those openings need to be plugged. Mics such as the Shure 520, 440, and the Astatic T-3 have openings that need to be closed to prevent sound waves from entering the mic's body and interacting with the rear of the CM and CR elements, causing feedback problems. This was first brought to my attention by Fritz years ago when I first brought my performing mics to him.

Mic & Amp Matching

Keep in mind that different amps "like" different mics. If you have an amp that is very distorted, try using a mic with a smoother, softer sounding element, like a dynamic or not-so-strong crystal. If you have an amp that doesn't distort enough for your taste, try a mic with a stronger element such as the Shure CM or CR, or the Astatic MC-151 crystal. If you like the tone of an amp, but feedback is a problem, you're either not cupping the mic well enough or the amp is being driven beyond its capabilities. "Tube Swapping" for tube amps can help and lowering how much gain you use ("Gain" volume, "Drive," or "Pre and Post" on some amps), as opposed to the normal volume, may help with these factors as well. The key is experimentation.

As a side note. I personally like the sound of the Shure CM or CR elements with my Fender amps. When performing on stage sometimes the tone I really like is too muddy to cut through and be heard. As a result, my sound gets lost in the mix of instruments. Playing through a brighter mic, like the Astatic JT-30 with a crystal element, may enable you to be heard better above the band. This is something to keep in mind: A fat, bassy tone from an amp and mic combo might sound good on its own, but with a band, it may get lost.

Vocal Mics & PA

For the non-blues player, or for the blues player looking for a cleaner tone, try playing through a cleaner mic. The Shure SM57 and SM58 microphones are high quality, very durable, and priced reasonably for their level of quality. These are standard professional vocal and instrumental mics. You can place them on a mic stand and play towards the mic's capsule, allowing you to do more hand sound-shaping effects with your hands. Hand held, these mics can be cupped as well, adjusting the amp for desired EQ.

Another good alternative to the basic bullet is the *Shaker Microphone*. They are small, light, come in dynamic and crystal configurations, and include a built-in volume control. These features also make them a good choice for a first harp mic as well as a backup to your main microphones.

Even smaller is the ***Finger Mic*** family. Finger mics are small, typically electret condensers or miniature dynamic mics, like those used as lapel mics or wireless systems for stage or TV. You can purchase a version of this mic for very little money at consumer electronic stores or spend lots of money on a higher-quality system at a pro audio outlet. For harmonica, either will work fine. Currently on the market is a mic system called the *Harmonica Honker*. This microphone incorporates a finger ring of which the mic is mounted along with a volume control. Many of these finger set-ups employ a belt-clip pre-amp and battery pack.

For blues players, a tube amp is pretty much a must-have. For cleaner tone, this may not necessarily be the rule. Suggestion: Take the mic you like and test it with as many amps as you can. You just might find that sometimes even a simple keyboard amp does a wonderful job. There are many pleasant surprises waiting to be discovered by the player willing to investigate. For further information on amps and effects refer to ***Harmonica Amps*** within this series.

Give Me The Facts!

What You NEED to know

I recommend that every blues harmonica player have these items at a gig.

1. One mic containing a Shure CM or CR element.
2. One mic with an Astatic crystal element
3. One of these mics with a volume control or on/off switch (not necessary, but very nice to have).
4. One cable for each mic (A back-up cable or adapter if both your mics use the same cable).
5. An amp loud enough so you can hear yourself on stage.
6. Extension cord, power strip, small flashlight, extra tubes, fuses, water, business cards, pen, CDs to sell, etc. Be prepared for anything. Have a gig bag or case outfitted that you take with you to each show. The one time you need it could prove to be crucial. My friend, guitarist John Garcia, even takes a soldering iron to his gigs. He's prepared!
7. A good cup on the microphone and an understanding of what techniques to use to achieve the tone and effect you are looking for (This is covered in Building Harmonica Technique Level 2 MB99107DVD & Building Harmonica Technique Level 3 MB9113DVD).

Many players assume a great mic and amp will give them the tone they're looking for. Wrong. Though these are helpful elements, nothing can take the place of good technique and experience. Assuming your skills and knowledge of technique (embouchure, tongue block slaps, pulls, pull-slaps, octaves, etc.) are pretty good, expect it to take a couple years of practicing with a mic and amp to become proficient at what is called the "amplified sound."

I don't mean to discourage anyone who is beginning this journey. These are just the realities of dealing with the complex subtleties of amplified harp. As a new performer you may place your judgment of an amp and mic combo on how it can make you sound at that moment. But... an amp and mic that may have sounded somehow lacking to you could prove to be the most exciting amp/mic combo a professional player has ever played through! There are many, many variables, not the least of which is the human factor.

My recommendation for you is to write a list of the professional players whose tone you like the most. Then, when seeing them performing live, look to see what gear they are using. Ask them (if they are available) to speak with you about their rig. Most players are happy to talk about the equipment they use, and most have formed strong opinions based on their experiences (from which you can benefit). Keep in mind that professional players will often use different mic and amp combos in the studio. Ask them what they use live and then what they like to use when recording. This will give you perspective when it comes time for you to record.

For More Information

I hope this has been helpful in your quest for the right mic for you. We have covered the most commonly used mics, of course there are more. Look at the Harmonica Masterclass Website at www.harmonicamasterclass.com and click on Vintage Collection. You will find a huge database of all types of microphones and amplifiers. Good luck and have fun!

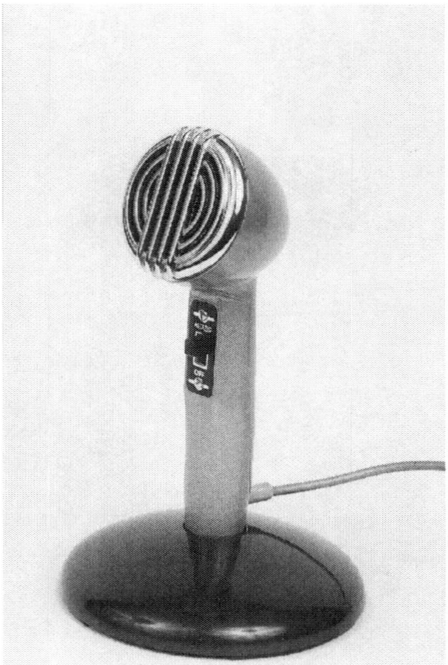

Astatic 200S with original metal base

Astatic T3

Astatic UT48

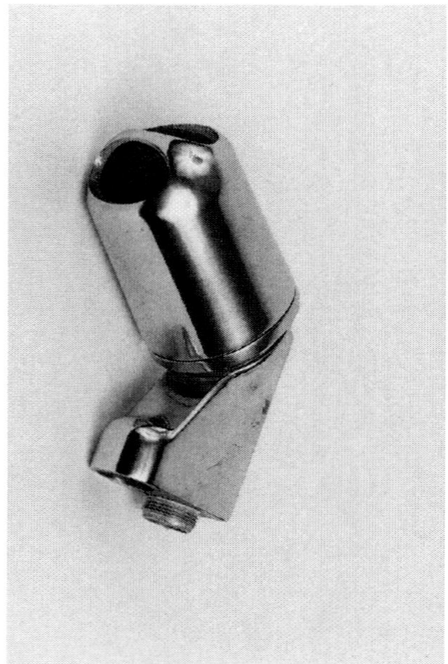

Electro-Voice 638

Smaller Shure "Brown Bullet" on its original wood stand and metal base.

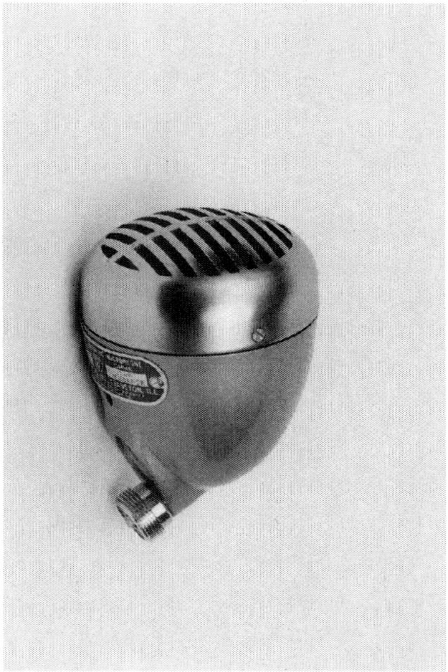

Shure 707A with a larger body and a custom screw-on output connector added.

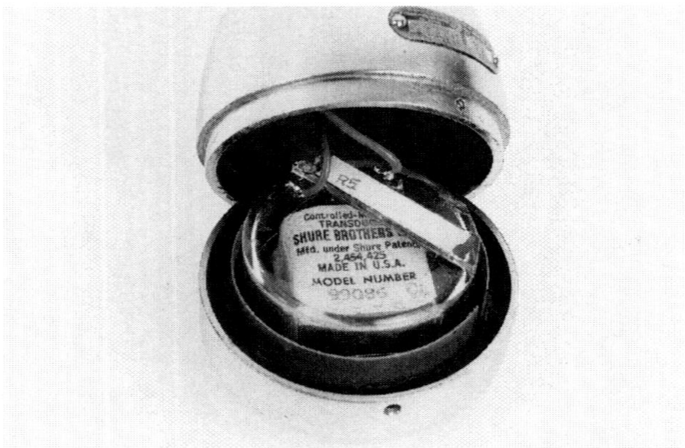

Shure R5 element in a
Shure 7A body

Harmonica Amplifiers

A BASIC GUIDE

by DAVID BARRETT

Live photo of David Barrett
by
Sarbajit Banerjea

Harmonica Amplifiers

The **Gig Savers®** series has been designed to give studying harmonica players answers to common questions in a brief, affordable, yet informative fashion. ***Harmonica Amplifiers*** is the first published book to specifically cover harmonica amplifiers and their usage. This is a subject of special interest to all players due to the lack of available information about the topic. Most players, like myself, have had to acquire many microphones and amplifiers before they found the right one(s) that match their sound. I have owned many different models of amplifiers and microphones and have gathered much useful information on the subject. This book is primarily written for the blues harmonica player, but most of the information is applicable for the non-blues player as well.

Please refer to the back of this book for a listing of other harmonica books available within this series. I would highly recommended purchasing the book ***Harmonica Microphones*** as well to round your knowledge of the subject, since the amplifier is only half of the equation for achieving tone.

I would like to thank Sonny Junior of Sonny Junior Amplifiers, Fritz Hasenpusch the Harp Mic Man, and Tom Ellis of Tom's Mics for their expert information and help through the years.

The Package

There are many aspects of an amp (and the mic you use with it) that can make it sound good or bad. Assuming you have a good amp, this all rests on the knowledge you have on what each of the components of the amp does and how to use them. Within this text we'll speak of each part of the amplifier and common ways in which they are used by professional players.

The Head

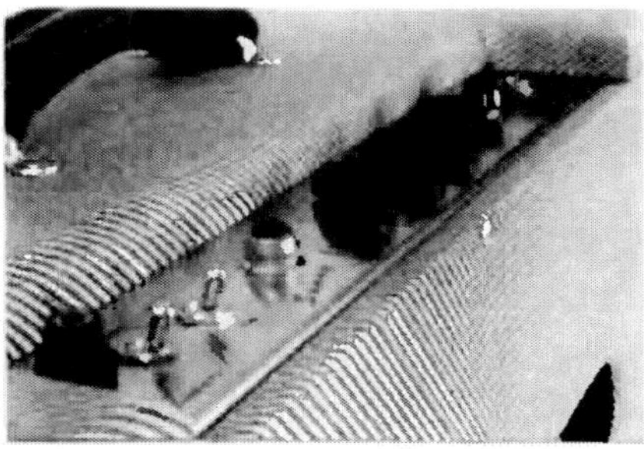

Input – You will sometimes have an option of where to plug in your microphone. If it's an older tube amp (~ 1950's), it might have an instrument input or microphone input. This one is easy, use the microphone input. Many amplifiers give you a choice of Low Gain, High Gain or Bright. All of these are OK; it's up to you which one sounds better for the microphone you're using and personal taste.

Clean Channel – Newer amps will often have two channels, one called "clean" and the other called "distortion." The clean channel introduces no artificial distortion and will have lower overall gain. Natural distortion through the clean channel is generally a good thing. This comes from using a microphone (usually a bullet microphone) tightly cupped to send an already distorted, muted

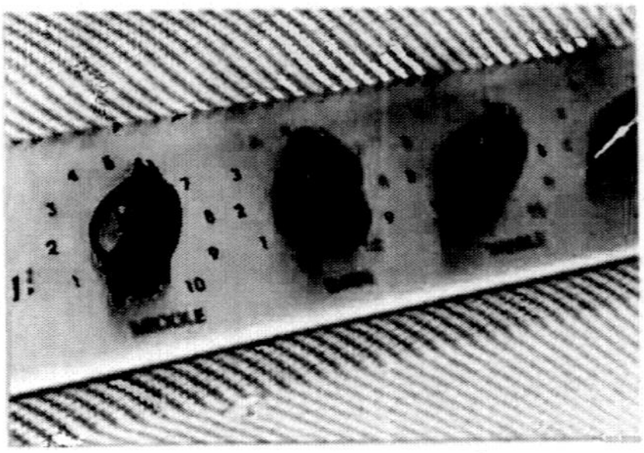

signal from which the amplifier tubes (pre-amp and power section) amplify to further warm up the tone. Cabinet and speaker size also go into the mix when speaking of tone. This channel will commonly have:

1. **Bass** – Used to cut (take away) or boost (add) more lows. For most amps, the harmonica player will turn this way up (6-10).
2. **Mid** – Used to cut or boost mids. For most amps, the harmonica player will turn this from 2-5.
3. **Treble** – Used to cut or boost highs. For most amps, the harmonica player will turn this from 0-4.
4. **Presence** – Used to cut or boost highs higher than the treble control. For most amps, the harmonica player will turn this from 0-4.
5. **Volume** – To control how loud the amp is.

Distortion Channel – Some amps, no matter what you do, just don't sound good on the clean channel. In this instance, you can use the distortion channel if available. This channel will commonly have:

1. **Gain** – Every amp uses different names for the distortion section. Sometimes amps don't have a seperate distortion section, but they do have a gain control. You can think of your gain control as a distortion control; the higher it is, the more distortion you get. When using the gain, you need to understand with most amps the gain and volume control are married together.

In most cases, you want the volume control higher, and the gain control lower. Too much gain will give you exces sive feedback and low volume.

2. **Pre-Gain/Post-Gain** – Pre-gain and post-gain work in much the same way as the gain and volume above. For most amps, turn your post-gain all the way up and use the pre-gain as your volume. If you want more distortion at a lower level, then mix them more evenly.
3. **Footswitch** – Most amps with two channels have a footswitch to switch you between the lead (distortion) and clean channel. You could use the clean channel for your background playing and have the lead channel dialed in to be a little bit louder and more distorted. When moving into a solo, you hit your foot pedal to switch channels and away you go. This is an option, but not commonly done by harp players.

Other Features

Effects Loop – Some amps have an in and out called an effects loop. When using an effects pedal (like reverb or delay), you normally plug your mic cable into the pedal and then run a cable into the input of the amp. Instead of doing that, you can use the effects loop and run a short cable from the "out" to the "in" of the pedal and run another short cable from the "out" of the pedal to the "in" of the effects loop. Either way of hooking up your pedal works, but each will have a little difference in tone.

Line Out – This output allows you to send a pre-amplified signal (called a line level signal) to another unit. This is commonly used to send a signal to the house (house PA system or recording studio) so that you don't have to use a microphone in front of the amp. This is an option, but most (if not all) players will prefer to mic their amp. The tone you hear from an amp comes from the head, cabinet and speakers combined. If you use the line out, you eliminate all the good the cabinet and the speakers provide. When micing an amp, place the microphone in front of your speaker, about one inch away, and one inch towards the center of the speaker from the edge.

Speaker Out – This output allows you to send an amplified signal to another speaker cabinet (cabinet with only speakers, no head). By using this output to run a second (besides the cabinet built into your amp) speaker cabinet, you can cover a larger area of the stage to be heard. Make sure the output impedance of the amp (see amp's specs) and the ohms rating of the cabinet (see cabinet's specs) are matched. Sometimes having a mismatched ohms rating is fine, but sometimes it can blow up your amp. Any amp you buy with a speaker out will tell which combinations of speakers you can use. Another note, never use the speaker out to send a signal to a mixer or other line-level input device, use the line out for this.

Headphones Out – This is great to use when practicing in an environment you need to be quiet. In most amplifiers the signal is cut to the speakers when plugging in your headphones.

Reverb – A great echo effect used by most players. The older amps use a spring reverb, with the newer amps using digital. Even though both work fine, spring reverb is preferred for the warmer tone and even decay.

Tremolo – Also seen on some amps as only "Speed" and "Intensity," this is an effect not usually used by harp players. This gives the player an amplitude modulation effect.

Speakers

Speaker size is also an important issue when purchasing an amp. Most harp players prefer 10" speakers. Most players use a 1X10" speaker size amp (like the old Fender Princeton amps) for small shows or recording, or the 4X10" speaker size amp like the Fender Bassman. The 10" speakers have good bass response, good mid presence and good high-end punch. The 10" speaker also has a good throw. This means that the amp can be heard from far away (the 4X10" model).

The 12" speaker size in amps of the 1950's I think sound great. Gibson amps, to name one brand, are very nice. The Fender amps that use 12" speakers I feel are a little too bright and stiff; they don't have the warmth of the smaller speakers.

Some amps, like the famed Sonny Jr. amps, use 8" speakers. The 8" speakers drive very well, and when coupled together (Sonny's amps use four or six 8" speakers) have good bass response. Though not as loud as the 10" or 12" speaker setups, they still do fine on stage.

On occasion you will see 15" speakers used. Again, the older amps sound pretty good, but the newer amps using 15" speakers usually don't sound too great.

Some amps incorporate a combination of speakers. On occasion you'll see on old amps 8", 10", 12" and 15" speakers mixed together in one cabinet. Another option is to use an extension cabinet with different speaker sizes. Again, the key word is to experiment!

Effects

Harmonica players have traditionally used reverb as the main stay of performance and recording. Delay (an echo-type effect) is also a great sounding effect used often.

An EQ is also a handy tool. The EQ (equalizer) is a unit that seperates the pitch spectrum further than what a normal amp has – bass, mid and treble. Some amps just have one EQ knob – tone. This EQ can help you better dial in what you want and don't want. Instead of the normal three controls, you can purchase a unit that gives you thirty areas of the frequency you can cut or boost. This is also helpful in reducing feedback. Some frequencies are more inherent to feeding back than others. An EQ allows you to find the thin slice of frequency that's feeding back and turn it down.

Also handy devices to have are a foot pedal volume control (if you don't have a volume control on your mic) and wireless unit. A wireless unit (usually we use guitar wireless and adapt it for our use) allows you to be cordless and walk among the audience. Very cool for strong stage performance. While in the audience you can also check to see how the band sounds, and more importantly, how you sound!

Tube Substitutions

If you have a tube amp, you are most likely going to want to experiment with different gain tubes. Amplifiers are rarely made for harmonica players. We are usually using guitar amps. These guitar amps are set up for guitars, not microphones. When playing through an amp, especially a Fender amp, you usually don't achieve good tone until you're VERY LOUD! And by then, you're feeding back so badly you can't play.

To remedy this problem with larger amps, we change the tubes to make the amp distort at a lower volume. How this is done is by making an amp less efficient. This is achieved by using lower gain tubes. Let's use a Fender '59 Reissue Bassman as an example. When I go on the road performing or teaching a Harmonica Masterclass Workshop® I usually ask a student from that area to bring a Bassman for me. When arriving, I make two changes. I change the rectifier from solid state to a 5U4 tube rectifier. This change lowers the plate voltage on the output tubes and thus reduces the gain and adds compression. I also change the rightmost (facing back of amp) pre-amp tube from a 12AX7 to a lower gain 12AY7. Here's the principle.

By replacing the higher gain tubes with lower gain tubes, you're making the amp work harder to create the same level of volume. This will give you better tone at a usable stage volume. This will give you better tone at a usable stage volume that is less prone to feedback. Commonly used pre-amp tubes (listed from lowest to highest gain) are: 12AU7, 12AY7, 12AT7 and 12AX7. 5Y3, 5AR4/GZ34, and 5U4 are the most commonly used rectifier tubes.

The mixture of pre-amp tubes also has a lot to do with the overall tone. I currently play through a Fender '59 Custom Bassman-like amplifier designed and built by Sonny Jr., I like his use of tube combinations. With the amps he sells, he even sends extra tubes and information on how they can be used to achieve differences in tone.

For smaller amps, in most cases, we want the amp to distort at a higher volume. Because it's a smaller amp, we want to get as much bang for the buck in volume as we can. In this case, the higher gain tubes are preferred. I run 12AX7's across the board with my 1972 Fender Princeton amp (10" speaker).

Again, the important thing to do is experiment with different combinations for all size amps. Most Fender amps are pretty friendly to tube changes. Most amps need to be rebiased after output tube (power tubes) changes though, with some using tubes with different socket types altogether. If you're not sure about something, visit your local amp shop (ask if they specialize in vintage amps) and ask some questions. You can probably pick up your tubes there as well.

Amp Size, Placement & Controlling Feedback

I am a strong believer in having an amp large enough to hear yourself on stage without monitors. If you can't hear yourself, you can't play. What you're fighting against is a loud drum set and a guitarist(s) who can play louder than we'll ever be able to play. Because we have a microphone in our hands, we are more prone to feedback.

One way to play a show is to use your favorite small to mid-size amp and run it through the house and monitors. This is done by micing your amp (they place a microphone in front of your amp's speaker to go to the PA system) and amplifying it through the main speakers of the house. This is for the audience to hear you well. A second signal is sent from the house to a set of monitors on stage for the performers to hear. If it's a sophisticated system, you will have your own monitor speaker (placed on the floor in front of you) in which you can tell the sound engineer who you want to hear through it. You will want mostly you and maybe a little vocals.

This is a good situation, but you have no physical control over the volume of that monitor. You will have to verbally or physically make a cue to the sound engineer (if he's looking) to turn you up or down. The best scenario is you do a sound check and all the levels are taken care of before the show. The problem with this is that stage volume changes throughout the night. The guitarist could turn up, the drummer might play stronger and you can't do anything to turn yourself up, because your little amp just won't play any louder. You can keep telling the engineer to turn you up, but you'll always reach the point where, even with monitors, you'll feedback and you physically can't get any louder.

In most cases you don't get your own monitor, you share a monitor with all the musicians on the front line (usually vocals and guitar). In this case, you usually won't be able to have enough of you through the monitors to hear yourself. The vocalist wants to hear him or herself without your loud harmonica coming through their monitor.

I paint a grim picture for smaller amps. In many cases they CAN work fine. Some players have played all their life on small amps and they have served them fine. My experience, and that of most pro players, is that it's safer to have a larger amp. Too many times when playing with a small amp I couldn't hear myself, was getting feedback and was overplaying (playing the harp too loud/hard) just to hear myself. When this situation comes up, you know you're going to walk off the stage with a whole bunch of dead harps.

Here is what I recommend for players with a semi-loud to loud band. Play an amp large enough to hear yourself with no monitors. When the sound guy comes up to mic your amp, ask him for a little monitors. This way you get a little bit of your sound through the monitors to hear yourself if you walk away from your amp during a hot trading of licks with the guitarist. But, it's not so loud that you have feedback problems or offend the other players using the same monitor.

Sonny Jr. recommends getting your amp off the floor by stacking two to three milk crates below your amp. This gets the amp at yours and the audience's ear level to be heard better.

The amp is usually placed behind us. If you're singing, the amp is behind you, and to the left or right a bit. The drummer, staged dead center back, is not going to want you to place your amp in front of his bass drum. Mark Hummel recommends that you face the amp a little towards you to hear better. Some players have also placed the amp on the left or right of them, facing directly at them. This is called a side fill. If you're not playing too loud, you can do this without feedback. Experiment with what works for you.

Give Me The Facts!

What You NEED to know

I recommend that every blues harmonica player have these items at a gig.

1. One mic containing a Shure CM or CR element.
2. One mic with an Astatic crystal element.
3. One of these mics with a volume control or on/off switch (not necessary, but very nice to have).
4. One cable for each mic (A back-up cable or adapter if both your mics use the same cable).
5. An amp loud enough so you can hear yourself on stage.
6. Extension cord, power strip, small flashlight, extra tubes, fuses, water, business cards, pen, CDs to sell, etc. Be prepared for anything. Have a gig bag or case outfitted that you take with you to each show. The one time you need it will save the night. My friend, guitarist John Garcia, even takes a soldering iron to his gigs. He's prepared!
7. A good cup on the microphone and an understanding of what techniques to use to achieve the tone and effect you are looking for (This is covered in Building Harmonica Technique Level 2 MB99107DVD & Building Harmonica Technique Level 3 MB9113DVD).

Most players assume a great mic and amp will give them the tone they're looking for. Wrong. Though these are helpful elements, nothing can take the place of good technique and experience. Assuming your skills and knowledge of technique (embouchure, tongue block slaps, pulls, pull-slaps, octaves, etc.) are pretty good, expect it to take a couple years of practicing with a mic and amp to become proficient at what is called the "amplified sound." I don't mean to discourage anyone; these are just the realities of dealing with the complex subtleties of amplified harp. As a new performer you may place your judgment of an amp and mic combo on how it can make you sound at that moment. But... an amp and mic that may have sounded lacking to you, may be the most exciting amp and mic combo a professional player has ever played through! There are many, many variables, not the least of which is the human factor.

My recommendation for you is to write a list of the professional players whose tone you like the most. Then, when seeing them performing live, look to see what gear they are using. Ask them (if they are available) to speak with you about their rig. Most players are happy to talk about the equipment they use, and most have formed strong opinions based on their experiences (from which you can benefit). Keep in mind that professional players will often use different mic and amp combos in the studio. Ask them what they use live and then what they like to use when recording. This will give you perspective when it comes time for you to record.

For More Information

I hope this has been helpful in your quest for the right amp for you. We have covered the most commonly used amps, of course there are more. Look at the Harmonica Masterclass Website at www.harmonicamasterclass.com and click on Vintage Collection. You will find a huge database of all types of microphones and amplifiers. Good luck and have fun!

First Harmonica Gig

EVERYTHING YOU NEED TO KNOW

A BASIC GUIDE

by DAVID BARRETT

Live photo of David Barrett
by
Sarbajit Banerjea

First Gig

Everything You Need to Know

The **Gig Savers®** series has been designed to give studying harmonica players answers to common questions in a brief, affordable, yet informative fashion. **First Gig** is the first published book to specifically cover what a harmonica player is to do from before he or she leaves the house until the gig is over. This is a subject of special interest to all players due to the lack of information about the topic. Most players, like myself, have had to just go out and experience this. I think this book will do a good job to help prepare you for this first big step. This book is primarily written for the blues harmonica player, but the ideas really apply across the board for any style that you wish to perform.

Please refer to the back of this book for a listing of other harmonica books available within this series. I would highly recommended purchasing the books ***Harmonica Amplifiers, Harmonica Microphones, Essential Theory, Essential Scales,*** and ***Essential Quick Charts*** as well to round your knowledge of the subject.

The Jam Session

Most players are going to cut their teeth at jam sessions for a while before playing with a band, so let's start here.

Before the Jam

Before going to the jam, there is some preparation that needs to take place.

Prepare Tunes – You'll want to have some classic songs that most players know under your belt. Assuming that you don't sing, you can still call vocal tunes on which you can play harp. I can't stress the fact that it needs to be a very common blues standard; otherwise, the house band (band that backs all of the jammers) won't know your tune. If you can sing, even better! There are no worries. An even safer bet is to learn some instrumentals. This way you can call any tune you wish as long as you can tell them the key, where it starts, what type of groove it uses, and count them in.

A song like Little Walter's "Juke" might be a good song to learn. This tune uses the standard twelve bar blues form in the key of E (A harmonica), it starts on the one chord and it's a medium shuffle. You can also choose to play an original instrumental. When I play a jam session and play an instrumental, all I have worked out is the head. The head is the first chorus (12 bars) of the song and usually the last chorus. The head is a very melodic, catchy chorus that makes the song interesting. After playing the head, you can proceed to improvise the middle of the song, hand the solo over to another jammer, take it back from them and repeat the head at the end to bring the song to a close. An instrumental sounds much more polished this way. You're playing a song, not just jamming.

Whatever you choose, have something ready. You could just play along to whatever is presented by the bandleader, but many times they ask you "what do you want to do?" If you have some experience with common blues songs, at least you'll have something to call. A well worked out vocal song or instrumental goes over very well.

I also highly recommend ALL players study how to play backup. Most players overlook this. Most students only study how to solo. Where your playing can really shine is in playing behind and within the fills of a song in a strong supportive manner. Purchase every Muddy Waters and Jimmy Rogers recording you can get your hands on. They both used fantastic harp players throughout their careers.

Amplifier & Microphone Choice – You will need to decide what amp and mic to take with you. Some jam sessions provide an amp and mic for you. Others just have an amp, and some nothing at all. If it's your first time at a jam, take your rig. If it stays in the back of your car because there's already something there, great, at least you were prepared.

I always like to take an amp large enough that I can hear myself without monitors, like a Fender Bassman. Most the time at a jam session you have only moments to set up. You can't count on having the house sound engineer there to mic your amp through the PA and run some of your sound into the monitors so you can hear yourself. If you don't own a large amp, you can bring your smaller amp, but ask the jam leader if you can set up during the break. This way there is more time to achieve a good volume on stage, either through monitors or placing your amp up high, closer to your ears.

The mic is easy. Take whatever mic sounds best with the amp you're bringing.

Harmonica Choice – The most common used harps to play Blues are; G, A, B♭, C and D. You could just take these. If your position knowledge (ability to play each harp in multiple keys) is strong, these are just fine. Though these will probably be just fine, it is good to have an assortment to make sure you can cover any keys that are called. Keep in mind that there will probably be singers, piano players and sax players at a jam. All of them can call keys that aren't as common to you.

Detailed below are all the available keyed harmonicas. The bottom harmonicas are lowest in pitch, with the top harmonicas being highest in pitch. The harmonicas in **bold** are what I usually take to a show. If you play the chromatic harmonica, of course bring that as well. The low harmonicas (Low D, Low C, etc.) are not necessary, but really nice to have. So many times a band calls a tune in C that you'll want to play in second position, but the F harmonica is too high and shrill for the song. Having a low F harmonica is a great alternative.

Recommended Harmonicas

High G
F-Sharp
F
E
E-Flat
D
D-Flat
C
B-Flat
A
A-Flat
G
Low F
Low E
Low E-Flat
Low D
Low C (Hohner 364/365)

Extras to Have – Definitely have water with you. This is the most important. It's also nice to have a towel to wipe your sweat if you're able to stay up for a while. Stage lights can make the stage very hot. I also recommend having an extension cord, power strip, flashlight, extra tubes, fuses, and anything else you can think of you'll need. Be prepared for the worst. Have a little gig bag that you take with you to each show; the one time you need it, it will save the night. My friend, guitarist John Garcia, even takes a soldering iron to his gigs. He's prepared!

Attitude – The players that get asked back the most are the ones with humility and know when it's time to be up front and play strong, and know when it's time to be in the background and play softly – or not at all. Always take the vantage point that the band is giving you the honor of playing with them. Be confident in your playing, no matter how strong a player you think you are, but ALWAYS keep in mind you are making music. When playing on stage, ask yourself "Am I playing just to play, or does what I'm playing sound good with the music?" If you follow this principle, you'll always do well.

Arriving at the Jam

All right, you're here and you're ready to go. Most jam sessions have a sign-up list. Spot the sign-up list and get on it as soon as possible. In many jams the sign-up list fills up the first twenty minutes of the night. After signing up, sit down with your gear and enjoy the show. Don't be upset if you don't get called up when you think you're supposed to be on. The person running the jam will read the crowd. If he or she feels a lull, they will call up someone they are familiar with to bring the mood up.

Don't drink too much, that can give you cotton mouth and make you want to go to the bathroom as you get up on stage. Nerves will do that.

You're Called Up – Here's the moment you've been waiting for. After being called up, spot the leader of the jam and ask where you can set up. After plugging in your amp, turning it on, and plugging in your mic, test your volume. Set the amp louder than you think you need it. The roar of the band quickly engulfs what you thought was a loud setting. If there is a soundman there, ask him to mic the amp. This is wanted for two reasons. One, no matter how large your amp is, you want your sound coming through the house speakers. This distributes your sound to be heard better. Two, you can ask to have a little bit of you through the monitors. Be careful to not have too much, you don't want to be feeding back on stage the whole time.

All right, you're all set up and ready to go. Make sure you have water near by. Don't set the water on your amp, the other musicians' amp, or on any sound system equipment. This is both dangerous and a BIG no no, especially on vintage amps worth more than the vehicle you drove to the show in.

When the Band Calls the Tune – At this time the song needs to be chosen. Either you will be asked to call a tune, or they will call the tune and tell you the key. If they choose the song, select the appropriate harmonica and wait for the count. I would recommend that you wait a moment before you play. Listen to the groove and see what the lead guitarist is going to do. Sometimes the lead guitarist fills all the holes, only leaving you with a solo in the middle. If you see that no one is taking the holes, you fill them. When it's your turn to solo, the bandleader will look up at you and nod just before the next chorus you are to solo in. Take your solo, giving him back the reins after you're done. Most soloists are given two times around (two choruses). Watch the jam closely before you go up. If you notice the bandleader getting restless after someone solos more than two times around, then you know that's how much solo you should take when it's your turn. If you see the bandleader is more open, you can solo as long as you want (within reason) until you have shared your musical moment with the audience.

When you're done, at the turnaround (the last two measures), look at the bandleader to let him or her know you're done. If you just keep playing with no signal and stop after the turnaround, there will be no one playing because you didn't tell anyone you were done with your solo. This is bad, don't do this. Performing music is about communication; make sure to make your intensions clear to the other band members.

Sometimes you will encounter a song with breaks. When a break is to happen, the bandleader will place his hand up, or behind him, where the band can see and hover for a moment. When his hand comes down, there will be a break. Watch closely for these. If there's a break, and you step into it, you'll sound foolish. When in doubt, sit out. Watch the band and play when it's safe. The next time the break comes around, you'll be ready for it.

When You Call the Tune – If you call the tune, you need to take charge. You are the bandleader and are responsible for making ALL the calls. First call the key. Example: G. Then tell them to the groove. Example: Shuffle. Tell them where the song starts. Example: From the one. Play the tune in your mind for a moment while tapping your foot to make sure your tempo is correct. Once you have the tempo locked in, start counting. Example: 1. 2. 1 2 3 4 start.

If the song has breaks, make the hand signals to call the breaks. If you want to give another instrument a solo, look at the person as you are finishing yours. Keep in mind you are the leader. If you aren't paying attention, the song can sound lost and sound to have no purpose. It is also your job to end the song. On your last solo, at the five chord (ninth measure), raise your hand to signal that the song will end. After playing your ending lick and the band holds that ever-so-familiar last chord, raise your hand in a big way and bring it down to stop the train.

Your Turn is Over

Look at each band member before leaving the stage and nod your head in appreciation for allowing you up to play with them. Take your equipment and water off the stage promptly. Don't leave the club too soon. This is your chance to have people come up and thank you for playing and maybe to meet other players that liked the way you sounded and want to jam. Besides coming to get some playing experience, meeting other players to play with on a more regular basis is really the main benefit of these jams. At my School of the Blues in San Jose California, we do jams every month for our students. This is an essential part of the learning process for them and they usually are able to find someone to buddy up with after a couple of jams.

I always say to my students at a jam session you have a 50% chance of walking away pretty happy with what you did and a 50% chance of walking away totally disgusted with yourself, usually leading to the thoughts of quitting your instrument. Jam sessions can be rough. So much of our self-esteem is tied to how well we play. The more you play at jam sessions, the better the end result is.

Most students practice songs to jam tracks that sound the same every time they play them. Playing the same song, to the same groove, with a live band will sound different with every band. Each member of the band is responsible for the feel that is presented. This will throw you off at first, making some parts of your solo not work. This is to be expected. When working out songs ahead of time, try them on many similar jam tracks and feels. This will help to ensure more flexibility with the performance of your song.

Your First Gig

This is a very exciting time. At a jam session you never know what you're going to get. But this is your band, your tunes, and you're ready to show the world what you've got. Here are some considerations to keep in mind.

Set List – You will have a set list of songs written out before the show. Order the songs in a manner in which you feel will have the biggest impact on the audience. Don't do four slow songs back to back. Break up the use of tempos, major and minor songs, the keys, and the subject matter. Always place your best tunes on the opening and ending of each set. Most sets are forty-five minutes, with a fifteen-minute break. Time your songs in practice to get an idea how long each of your songs are. Know your songs well enough to allow spontaneity to happen on stage.

A specific note to you as a harmonica player: Don't play second position all night. Too much of one way of playing gets old fast. Break up the night with third and first position playing on the diatonic and try to use the chromatic on occasion. I try to play in all three positions each set. This is a personal challenge for me and I know it presents a more interesting pallet of colors for the audience. Incorporate this into your set list.

What to Bring

Every successful musician knows that you don't make your money from what the house pays; it's made from selling CDs, T-shirts, posters, etc. This being your first gig, you probably won't have any of this, but keep this in mind for the future. Also keep in mind that if you do have CDs and you sell very little at a show, you didn't come across to the audience very well. Your set material either wasn't strong enough, or you didn't present or connect well with your audience. This is hard to deal with, but always look for ways to connect with your audience without sacrificing your artistic values.

Bring business cards with you for possible new contacts from the show. Have a pen readily available and make sure, as the band-leader, to have some songs where the band plays without you so you can be available at times during the show to speak to people. Bring water, maybe a change of clothes if you're getting dressed up and anything else you can think of without packing too heavy.

PA Basics

When booking any show, ask if a PA and sound person are on site. If not, you need to bring one. It's a good idea for any band, especially if you wish to do private or corporate (these pay the best) shows to have a PA.

Here are the basics of what you need.

1. Microphones: You will need as many microphones, microphone stands and cables as there are band members. A common set up would be:
   a. Vocals: One mic (unless there is more than one singer or some songs use back-up vocals.)
   b. Harmonica: One mic to be placed in front of your amp.
   c. Guitar: One mic to mic the amp.
   d. Bass: One mic to mic the amp or a direct box to send a signal to the mixing board from the bass player's head.
   e. Drums: One microphone for the snare, one for the kick, and at least one over-head mic to pick up the toms and cymbals.
2. Mixer: This takes the signal from each of the microphones and allows you to control the volume of each of the individual instruments and the overall volume of the band through the main speakers and monitors. If you have the set-up as described above, you will need an eight-channel board, one channel for each instrument. It's also good to leave one channel free to run a CD player through to play songs during breaks.

3. Effects: An effects processor can be hooked up through the mixer to add reverb, delay, and any other effects you wish to have for the individual instruments.
4. EQ: From the mixer, a stereo signal is sent to an equalizer (EQ). The equalizer is used to help balance the over-all sound. Some rooms are very bassy; this can be fixed by cutting back the low frequencies. Some rooms have a tendency to feed back at certain frequencies; the EQ can help with this as well. There will usually be two EQ's, one for the main speakers and one for the monitor speakers.
5. Power Amp: The signal from the EQ's are then sent to the power amps. These provide the power needed to drive the speakers and monitors.
6. Speakers: From the main power amp your signal is sent to a pair of speakers, each with at least a 15" speaker and a tweeter. You will need speaker cables (50' is usually fine) to run to your power amp. Speaker stands are also nice to get them off the floor. These speakers provide the sound for the audience.
7. Monitor Speakers: A seperate signal is sent from the mixing board to an EQ and then to a power amp to run the monitors. These monitors are placed on stage for the band members to hear themselves. On more expensive systems, each player (or group of players) can have their own monitor mix, thus choosing whom they want and don't want to hear through their monitor.

This is a basic run through of what makes a PA work. You can get more expensive systems, but they are hard to manage on the road or when playing a show with a quick set up and tear down time window. Many bands use what's called a top-box. This is a self-contained system with mixer, effects, EQ, and power amp. These are much simpler and less expensive, and in most cases do the job just fine.

Keep your stage volume low. It's so easy to get into the mindset that louder is better. It isn't. You won't be able to hear the nuances on stage presented by the other musicians and the audience is probably wearing earplugs because of it. If you start loud, you have nowhere to go. If you start at a moderate volume, when you want to scream in a solo, you can.

Closing Thoughts

Music is wonderful. The making of music and sharing it with others is even better. Always keep in mind it's about the music and the story it tells to the listeners. Don't play harmonica, play music. If you keep this in mind, no matter your skill level, you'll do well. Good luck and have fun!

WWW.MELBAY.COM